This workbook is cross-referenced to the revision guide, *OCR GCSE Additional Applied Science A*, published by Lonsdale.

The questions and activities in this book will help to reinforce your understanding of the six modules on the OCR GCSE Additional Applied Science A specification (J632), from the Twenty First Century Science suite, providing excellent preparation for your exams.

You will have to sit three exams in total. The modular test papers are likely to include questions that require you to apply your scientific knowledge to interpret information and data. The questions on pages 85–96 of this workbook have been specially designed to allow you to practise these skills.

This workbook is suitable for use by Foundation and Higher Tier students.

> **HT** Any material that is limited to Higher Tier appears inside a grey tinted box, clearly labelled with the symbol **HT**.

A Note to Teachers

The pages in this workbook can be used as…

- classwork sheets – students can use the revision guide to answer the questions
- harder classwork sheets – students study the topic and then answer the questions without using the revision guide
- easy-to-mark homework sheets – to test students' understanding and reinforce their learning
- the basis for learning homework tasks which are then tested in subsequent lessons
- test material for topics or entire units
- a structured revision programme prior to the objective tests / written exams.

Answers to these worksheets are available to order.

ISBN 10: 1-905129-72-6
ISBN 13: 978-1-905129-72-0

Published by Lonsdale, a division of Huveaux Plc

Project Editor: Charlotte Christensen

Authors / Editors: Nathan Goodman, Eliot Attridge, Rebecca Skinner

Cover and Concept Design: Sarah Duxbury

Designer: Anne-Marie Taylor

Acknowledgements

IFC   ©iStockphoto.com / Andrei Tchernov
p.89   Data provided by the Forensic Science Service Ltd
p.90   ©National Oceanic and Atmospheric Administration / Department of Commerce

Contents

Contents

Life Care

1 Many organisations work together to ensure effective life care for patients and clients. Explain what is meant by the term **life care**.

....

....

....

2 Explain the difference between the NHS and private healthcare, in terms of cost to the patient.

....

....

....

3 Give two examples of local organisations that ensure life care for patients.

a) .... **b)** ....

4 List three reasons why clients might use the facilities at a fitness centre.

a) ....

b) ....

c) ....

5 List three functions that the management of the NHS needs to carry out in order for the organisation to work effectively.

a) ....

b) ....

c) ....

HT **6** Explain, in as much detail as possible, why there is always a conflict about spending within the NHS.

....

....

....

1 Briefly explain what a **practitioner** is.

....

....

2 Suggest four functions that a registered nurse might perform.

a) .... **b)** ....

c) .... **d)** ....

3 Fill in the spaces in the sentences below to explain the role of a fitness instructor.

A fitness instructor is trained to plan a .... of .... to meet

the client's .... and .... They will keep records of the

.... and take account of any .... needs.

4 It is important for health or fitness practitioners to have certain characteristics. Write **true** or **false** alongside each of the characteristics below as appropriate.

A health and fitness practitioner should…

a) become lifelong friends with the patient. ....

b) have good written, but poor communication, skills. ....

c) have empathy, patience and tact. ....

d) develop a detached yet personal relationship with the patient. ....

e) consider the whole life of the patient. ....

f) only understand how the brain works. ....

5 Suggest two ways in which health issues can be brought to the public's attention.

a) .... **b)** ....

6 Explain the long-term benefits, in terms of cost, of public information campaigns.

....

....

Life Care

1 List five factors that a practitioner needs to know about a patient before a diagnosis can be made.

a) .... b) ....

c) .... d) ....

e) ....

2 What is meant by the term **symptoms**?

....

3 Name three conditions that smokers are more likely to develop than non-smokers.

a) .... b) .... c) ....

4 Why can taking more than one type of medication at the same time be dangerous? Suggest three reasons.

a) ....

b) ....

c) ....

5 The amount of physical activity that a person undertakes can affect their health. Give three conditions or problems that could be caused by lack of exercise.

a) ....

b) ....

c) ....

6 Name two organs that can be affected by excessive alcohol consumption.

a) .... b) ....

HT **7** Explain, in as much detail as possible, why a patient must be properly assessed before a diagnostic test is carried out.

....

....

1 Describe, in as much detail as possible, how a pulse rate is taken.

....

....

2 Bill normally has a resting pulse rate of 70 beats per minute. He goes to his doctor one day because he is feeling unwell, and his resting pulse rate is measured at 55 beats per minute. His blood pressure is normal, and he has not suffered any recent shocks. What could his pulse rate be an indicator of?

....

3 Explain what is meant by the term **blood pressure**.

....

4 There are two values associated with blood pressure – **systolic** blood pressure and **diastolic** blood pressure. Explain what these two values represent.

....

....

....

5 Name two instruments that are used to measure blood pressure.

a) .... b) ....

6 A patient goes to see the doctor to have her blood pressure taken. The average of her three readings is $\frac{165}{95}$.

Does she have low, normal or high blood pressure? ....

7 Having high blood pressure is dangerous. Explain why.

....

....

8 Give three ways in which body temperature can be measured.

a) .... b) ....

c) ....

Life Care

9 A patient has his temperature taken and the reading is 35°C. What could this temperature be an indicator of?

....

....

10 How is aerobic fitness measured?

....

....

11 a) Use the Body Mass Index formula to calculate the BMI for the following people (show your workings):

  i) A girl who is 1.74m tall and weighs 130kg. ....

  ii) A male athlete who is 1.70m tall and weighs 57kg. ....

  iii) A fifty-year old lady who is 1.65m tall and weighs 100kg. ....

  b) Use the BMI chart opposite to determine whether the patients in part **a)** are underweight, the ideal weight or overweight.

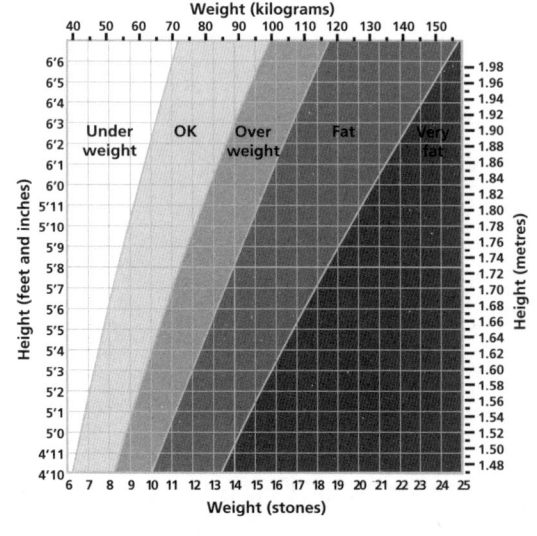

  i) ....

  ii) ....

  iii) ....

12 The body mass index is only a guideline. Give two reasons why it is not definitive. (Hint: think about factors that are not taken into account.)

....

....

13 Give two reasons why it is important to record and store patients' data.

  a) ....

  b) ....

1 The text below describes the procedure used to take a blood sample. The steps are in the wrong order. Number them 1 to 5 to put them into the correct order.

a) The syringe is inserted into a vein. ☐

b) The vacuum in the syringe draws in the required amount of blood. ☐

c) The skin is sterilised with an antiseptic wipe. ☐

d) The blood is sent for analysis. ☐

e) Pressure is applied to the arm in order to stop the bleeding. ☐

HT

2 Apart from blood and urine, name four other substances that can be taken from the body and analysed in order to help diagnose a patient's condition.

a) .... b) ....

c) .... d) ....

3 Explain how a urine test stick works.

....

....

....

4 What is the disadvantage of using a test stick to check urine? (Hint: think about what kind of test it is.)

....

HT

5 What is the name of the hormone that pregnancy test kits test for?

....

6 Draw lines to connect each of the substances found in urine or blood to its correct diagnosis.

Protein in urine	Could indicate diabetes
Blood in urine	Could indicate kidney damage or disease
Too much glucose in blood	Could indicate anaemia
Too much haemoglobin in blood	Could indicate a disease of the kidney, urinary system or bladder

Life Care

1 List two circumstances in which an X-ray image would be taken.

a) ....

b) ....

2 The scan below shows a developing fetus at 3 months old.

a) What imaging technique would have been used to take this image? ....

b) Explain why this imaging technique would have been used, and not an X-ray.

....

HT

3 Write down the names of three imaging techniques, other than X-rays and ultrasound, and give a use for each one.

a) ....

....

....

b) ....

....

....

c) ....

....

....

Life Care

1 There is a risk involved with any treatment. Explain why.

_____

_____

2 What do drug manufacturers have to include, by UK law, on or inside drug packaging?

_____

_____

3 Before a patient is given a course of drugs as a treatment, their informed consent needs to be obtained. What does the term **informed consent** mean?

_____

_____

4 a) A patient complains of repeatedly sneezing when she comes into contact with cats. Briefly describe the patient's symptom and suggest what the problem might be.

Symptom: _____

Problem: _____

b) Explain why treating the patient's symptom will not cure the problem.

_____

_____

5 The following people are admitted to an emergency ward. Number the boxes 1 to 4 to indicate the order in which they should be seen / treated.

a) A man suffering from food poisoning who is vomiting. ☐

b) A woman who is having a heart attack. ☐

c) A boy who has got a small bead stuck up his nose. ☐

d) A woman, who has been involved in a car accident, with possible broken bones and internal injuries. ☐

HT

6 a) What does NICE stand for? _____

b) Briefly describe the role of NICE.

_____

_____

_____

Life Care

1 Depending on the diagnosis of a condition, different treatments can be suggested. Suggest a suitable treatment(s) for the following conditions.

a) A patient who is overweight. ....

b) A serious knee injury. ....

c) A suspected allergy to dairy products. ....

2 Surgery could help to improve the health of a patient. What do surgeons have to weigh up before deciding whether to carry out surgery to treat a patient?

....

....

3 Exercise regimes may help to solve a patient's health problems. List three things that could be improved as a result of following an exercise regime.

a) .... **b)** .... **c)** ....

4 Zach has been told by his doctor that he must lose weight and needs to begin a fitness regime. However, Zach does not think that his weight is a problem and he finds exercise very boring. Do you think the exercise regime is likely to be effective for Zach? Give reasons for your answer.

....

....

....

5 Give two reasons why an individual might decide to change his / her diet.

a) ....

b) ....

HT **6** What is drug therapy? ....

....

7 Public Health Campaigns are run to make the public aware of a problem. Briefly list the main points that you think would be effective in a public health campaign which aims to make people aware of the problems of obesity.

....

....

1 What does a physiotherapist specialise in?

....

2 A physiotherapist needs to have a good understanding of how the body works. Explain why.

....

....

....

3 Briefly describe four steps that could be taken in an exercise programme to strengthen and treat an injured leg.

Step 1: ....

Step 2: ....

Step 3: ....

Step 4: ....

4 Explain why a patient's progress should be monitored during a fitness or training programme.

....

5 Give two reasons why a fitness programme may be modified during treatment. Explain your reasons.

a) ....

....

....

b) ....

....

6 Explain how a patient's fitness or training programme can be monitored...

a) during training ....

....

b) after completion of training. ....

....

Life Care

1 The diagram below shows a cross-section of the human heart.

a) On the diagram label the...

    i) right ventricle

    ii) left atrium

    iii) right atrium

    iv) left ventricle.

b) On the diagram mark the...

    i) vessel which carries blood from the lungs (with an A)

    ii) vessel which takes blood to the lungs (with a B)

    iii) vessel which takes blood to the body (with a C)

    iv) vessel which carries blood from the body (with a D).

2 Why do the ventricles have larger, more muscular walls than the atria?

3 The heart can beat at different rates, depending on certain factors. Give three factors that could cause the heart to beat at different rates.

a) .... **b)** .... **c)** ....

4 What does an **electrocardiogram** (ECG) monitor? Briefly explain how it works.

5 Name the three types of blood vessel that transport blood around the human body.

a) .... **b)** .... **c)** ....

6 Of the three blood vessels, which one allows substances to pass through the vessel wall?

1 The diagram below shows the human breathing system. Using the words below, correctly label their position on the diagram.

Alveoli   **Bronchiole**   **Bronchus**   **Diaphragm**

Lung   **Rib**   **Trachea**   **Intercostal muscles**

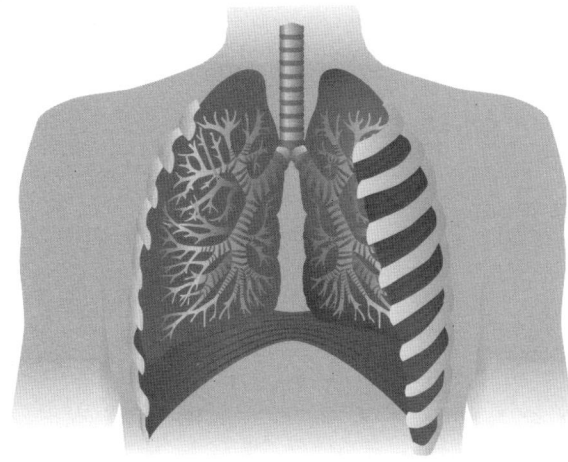

2 Explain how the structure of the trachea (windpipe) enables it to perform its function.

....

....

3 Describe, in as much detail as you can, how air is inhaled (taken in) and exhaled (moved out). (Use the words **lungs**, **thorax**, **ribcage** and **diaphragm** in your answer.) Sketch diagrams to help explain your answer.

....

....

....

....

Life Care

1 When blood is left to settle it separates into different components. List three components of the blood.

a) .... b) .... c) ....

2 a) Explain the role of red blood cells.

....

b) Why are red blood cells biconcave in shape?

....

3 a) Explain the role of the white blood cells.

....

b) Give two different ways in which white blood cells carry out their role.

....

....

4 What is the role of platelets?

....

5 Describe two purposes of the human skeleton.

a) ....

b) ....

6 a) Explain the function of bones, tendons, muscles and ligaments.

....

b) Explain how they all work together.

....

....

7 The diagram alongside shows the human skeleton.
Using the words below, correctly label the skeleton.

Clavicle	**Femur**
Pelvis	**Radius**
Skull	**Sternum**
Fibula	**Humerus**
Ribs	**Scapula**
Tibia	**Ulna**
Vertebral column	

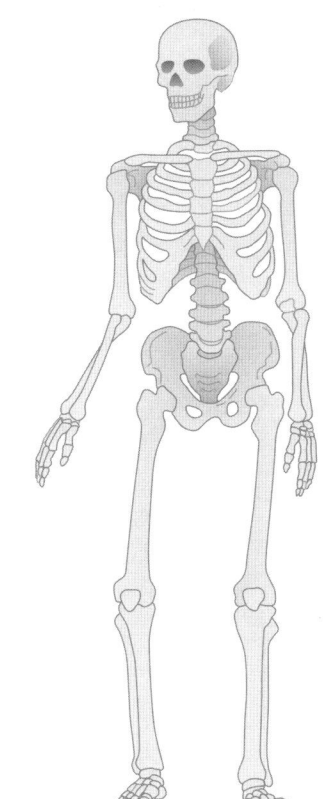

8 What is the role of the female reproductive system?

....

9 Using the words provided, correctly label the diagram of the female reproductive system below.

Cervix	**Fallopian tube**	**Ovary**	**Uterus**	**Vagina**

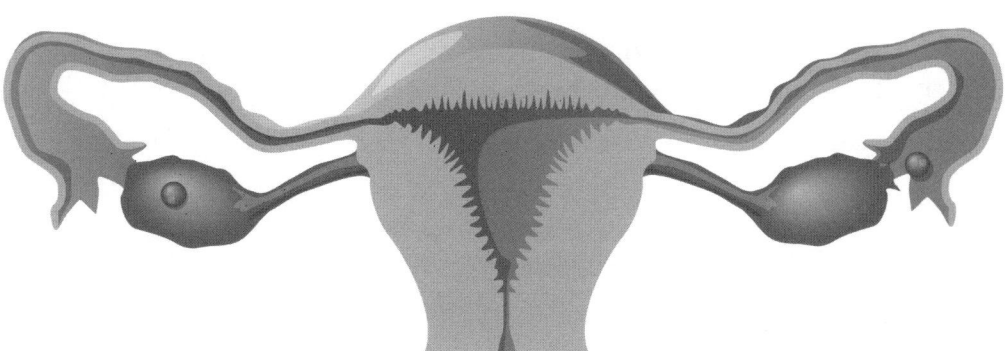

10 What is the function of the uterus?

....

Life Care

1. Briefly explain what happens during, and after, human fertilisation.

   ....

   ....

   ....

2. How long does an average pregnancy last in humans?

   ....

3. Several changes take place in the female reproductive system during pregnancy. List four of these changes.

   a) ....

   b) ....

   c) ....

   d) ....

4. Explain the function of the umbilical cord.

   ....

   ....

   ....

5. Explain the function of the placenta.

   ....

6. a) There are three stages of labour (giving birth). The first stage involves the baby's head aligning with the cervix. At this stage, by how much does the cervix dilate?

   ....

   b) What happens during the second stage of labour?

   ....

   c) What happens during the third stage of labour?

   ....

   ....

1 Give two health problems which may occur if the core body temperature becomes higher or lower than 37°C.

a) ....

b) ....

2 The two diagrams below show a blood vessel and a sweat gland in the skin at different temperatures.

A

Superficial capillary →

Shunt vessel

B

Superficial capillary →

Shunt vessel

a) Which diagram, A or B, shows the skin in hot conditions? ....

b) Explain, in as much detail as possible, how the body reacts if the temperature gets too low.

....

....

....

....

3 The kidneys control the balance of water in the body. Name the waste chemical filtered by the kidneys.

....

4 Fill in the gaps in the sentences, which describe how the kidneys balance the levels of chemicals in the body. Use the words in bold to help you.

bladder   filter   urine   salt   respiration   excrete   blood   sugar

The kidneys .... small molecules from the .... to form

.... (water, salt and urea). They absorb all the .... for

.... and as much .... as the body requires. The kidneys

.... the remaining urine which is stored in the ....

Agriculture and Food

1 Products can be harvested in different ways. Give the names of two types of harvest, and describe the process in each one.

a) ....

b) ....

2 In the wordsearch below find the names of 13 different products that can be harvested by either of the methods listed in question 1.

B	O	S	O	I	O	H	R	T	S	P	O	T	N	N
Y	O	E	T	B	F	E	T	E	N	E	T	O	H	S
N	P	N	A	R	H	S	L	I	U	O	R	E	E	O
E	Q	E	E	T	V	P	E	S	T	U	G	E	S	D
B	Y	U	A	M	P	H	F	U	S	G	T	E	F	X
T	I	E	O	A	E	E	A	G	S	D	T	I	A	F
T	L	T	M	R	L	A	W	A	D	O	G	T	A	Y
E	T	I	G	N	N	O	L	R	M	E	A	T	P	J
C	L	D	E	T	T	N	O	R	E	H	E	A	A	D
K	H	D	T	D	R	H	T	W	W	R	E	Y	O	O
N	I	S	O	M	Y	H	C	T	S	I	T	N	C	H
T	P	S	F	E	N	N	T	F	B	S	H	O	U	T
U	Y	S	A	C	E	A	I	H	D	I	T	E	N	N
O	E	P	E	A	R	S	T	I	A	T	H	W	M	R
N	W	E	O	T	U	O	R	A	N	G	E	S	N	A

3 Organisms can be used in many processes. List two examples.

a) ....

b) ....

4 Briefly explain the different stages of food production that are illustrated in a food chain.

....

....

....

1 **a)** Regulatory organisations are used to control agriculture and food production. Give three purposes of these organisations.

i) ....

ii) ....

iii) ....

b) Give the names of two of these regulatory organisations.

i) .... ii) ....

2 Give the names of two organisations that support a particular part of the food industry.

a) .... b) ....

HT

3 **a)** What is the aim of the Milk Development Council?

....

b) What is the purpose of ADAS?

....

4 Give the names of two crop plants that people can eat.

a) .... b) ....

5 Animals can be fed from the products of organisms. Name two examples of these products.

a) .... b) ....

6 Name two examples of food ingredients which are derived from plants.

a) .... b) ....

7 Unscramble the anagrams below to reveal products that can be made from plants.

a) NEILN .... **b)** LOHCOAL ....

c) PRAPE .... **d)** ODOW ....

e) NOTCOT .... **f)** ISELOBDIE ....

Agriculture and Food

1 a) Briefly explain what happens during the pollination of flowering plants.

_____

_____

b) In which two ways can the pollen be transferred from plant to plant?

i) _____ **ii)** _____

2 Briefly explain what happens during the fertilisation of plants.

_____

_____

3 a) Why do seeds and fruit have to be dispersed?

_____

b) List three ways in which seeds and fruit can be dispersed.

i) _____

ii) _____

iii) _____

4 a) Write down the equation for calculating seed germination.

_____

b) For each of the following, work out the germination rate. Show your working.

i) 150 seeds planted, 67 germinated. _____

ii) 200 seeds planted, 0 germinated. _____

iii) 180 seeds planted, 154 germinated. _____

iv) 205 seeds planted, 87 germinated. _____

v) 125 seeds planted, 98 germinated. _____

1 Name three factors that need to be balanced in a growing medium to ensure the optimum growth of a plant.

a) ....

b) ....

c) ....

2 List the two growing mediums that plants can be grown in.

....

....

3 a) Briefly explain how plants make their own food.

....

....

b) Complete the diagram below to show the inputs and outputs involved in photosynthesis.

c) Write the word equation for photosynthesis.

....

HT

4 List three factors that can limit the rate of photosynthesis.

a) ....

b) ....

c) ....

Agriculture and Food

1 **a)** Briefly explain the difference between a glasshouse and a polytunnel.

....

b) Explain how glasshouses and polytunnels can increase the growth of crops.

....

2 **a)** When crops are grown in a glasshouse, there are two methods by which insects pests can be minimised. List these two methods and explain how they work.

Method 1: ....

....

Method 2: ....

....

b) There are advantages and disadvantages to the methods listed in part **a)**. For each statement below, identify which type of pest control it is, and say whether it is an advantage or disadvantage (the first one has been done for you.)

i) The pests may be killed very quickly. .... **Chemical pest control, advantage**

ii) The pests may damage a large amount of the crop before the control works.

....

iii) Chemical residues may remain on the crop or be washed into streams and rivers.

....

3 **a)** Crop yield can be measured by finding the **wet mass**. How is wet mass found?

....

b) Give an example of a crop that can be measured using this method. ....

HT **4** What is the difference between the wet mass and dry mass of a product?

....

....

....

HT

5 **a)** What is a **clone**?

_____

b) By which two methods can a plant be cloned?

i) _____

ii) _____

6 Explain the differences between organic and intensive farming, in the way that animals are reared.

_____

_____

_____

7 Why might there be ethical concerns over rearing animals intensively?

_____

_____

_____

8 There are advantages and disadvantages to both organic and intensive farming methods. For each statement below, identify which farming method it is, and say whether it is an advantage or disadvantage (the first one has been done for you.)

a) Lower yield. _____ **Organic farming method, disadvantage**

b) Higher yield. _____

c) There may be ethical issues concerning the way animals are looked after. _____

d) The product commands a higher price. _____

9 Unscramble the anagrams below to find the five main factors that affect animal growth.

a) TREELHS _____   **b)** DFOO _____

c) PTMEETEUARR _____   **d)** AWTRE _____

e) ESSTP _____

Agriculture and Food

1 a) In which part of a male animal's body is sperm produced?

_____

b) In which part of a female animal's body are the ova produced?

_____

2 a) What is the name for the special type of cell division that produces gametes?

_____

b) If the number of chromosomes in a normal body cell is 38, how many chromosomes will there be in a gamete? Explain your answer.

_____

3 a) Explain in as much detail as you can, what happens during the process of fertilisation.

_____

_____

_____

_____

b) What is the name of the cell that is produced by fertilisation?

_____

4 Where does development of the embryo take place?

_____

5 Explain what is meant by the term **gestation period**.

_____

6 What happens to an animal after it has been born?

_____

1 What is the difference between artificial insemination and selective breeding?

....

....

2 Give two reasons why a farmer may want to control the time of breeding in cows.

a) ....

b) ....

3 Describe the four steps involved in the process of artificial insemination.

Step 1: ....

....

Step 2: ....

....

Step 3: ....

....

Step 4: ....

....

HT **4** In what circumstances would hormones be given to a cow?

....

5 **a)** Explain the advantage of selectively breeding animals.

....

....

b) Give an example of the result of selectively breeding animals.

....

Agriculture and Food

1 a) Explain, in as much detail as possible, how and when a surrogate mother is used during animal reproduction.

....

....

....

....

....

b) What is the advantage of using a surrogate mother?

....

2 Microorganisms can be used to produce food. Name two foods that that can be made using yeast.

a) ....

b) ....

3 a) What product is *Lactobacillus* used to make?

....

b) Name two other products that can be made using bacteria.

i) ....

ii) ....

4 *All microorganisms can be used in the production of food, and all are harmless.*
Is this statement **true** or **false**? Explain your answer.

....

....

HT **5** What is the name for disease-causing microorganisms?

....

© Lonsdale

1 The following steps describe the process of beer fermentation; they are not in the correct order. Number them 1–5 to put them into the correct order.

a) The yeast ferments the sugars, releasing CO_2 and alcohol. ☐

b) Malted barley is soaked in hot water to release the malt sugars. ☐

c) When the main fermentation is complete, the beer is bottled with a little bit of added sugar to provide the carbonation. ☐

d) The malt sugar solution is boiled with hops (for flavouring). ☐

e) The solution is cooled and yeast is added to begin the process of fermentation. ☐

2 Mycoprotein is a meat substitute. Number the steps 1 to 5 to put them into the correct order so they describe the process of mycoprotein fermentation.

a) The cycle starts again. ☐

b) A pure culture of fungus is added. ☐

c) The fungus is harvested. ☐

d) A nutrient broth is added to the culture vessel. ☐

e) The fungal hyphae (string-like filaments that increase surface area) grow. ☐

3 a) How does aerobic respiration release energy?

_____

b) Write the word equation for aerobic respiration.

_____

c) Anaerobic respiration takes place in the absence of oxygen. Write down the word equation for anaerobic respiration in yeast.

_____

4 a) In a fermentation process, approximately how long does the first stage of brewing last? _____

b) During that time, what process is taking place? _____

Agriculture and Food

1 Explain why sterile conditions must be used when culturing specific microorganisms.

....

HT **2 a)** The graph opposite shows the culturing of microorganisms. Label the graph to show the different stages that the microorganisms go through.

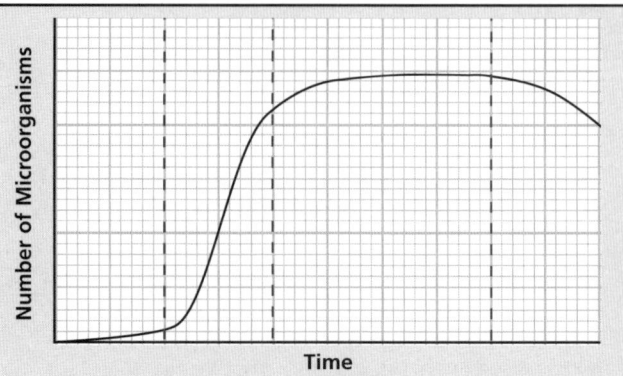

b) For each of the phases labelled in part **a)**, explain what happens to the microorganism population.

....

....

....

....

3 What is meant by the term **genetic modification**?

....

4 Give one example of the use of genetic modification to produce a useful product.

....

....

HT **5 a)** What is DNA?

....

b) Explain, using a specific example, how a gene can be genetically modified.

....

....

....

1 Explain what is meant by the term **batch culture**.

....

2 Explain what is meant by the term **continuous culture**.

....

3 In the wordsearch opposite, find the 5 factors that are needed when culturing microorganisms in a batch culture. Write them in the spaces below.

E	E	O	R	H	A	N	R	S	R	E
N	U	R	B	N	E	E	T	S	R	T
N	O	W	U	H	S	N	D	U	S	H
P	O	I	N	S	E	A	T	F	S	G
W	E	Y	T	I	S	A	E	O	R	I
Y	C	M	R	A	R	E	O	D	A	L
U	E	T	H	E	R	E	R	O	T	E
F	U	E	P	L	R	E	T	P	E	S
N	T	M	N	L	A	F	A	T	N	A
S	E	A	M	E	M	I	T	H	I	E
T	E	S	O	D	Y	A	A	L	C	G

a) ....

b) ....

c) ....

d) ....

e) ....

4 a) Give one advantage of using a batch culture rather than a continuous culture.

....

b) Give one advantage of using a continuous culture rather than a batch culture.

....

5 The diagram below shows a fermenter. Correctly label the diagram.

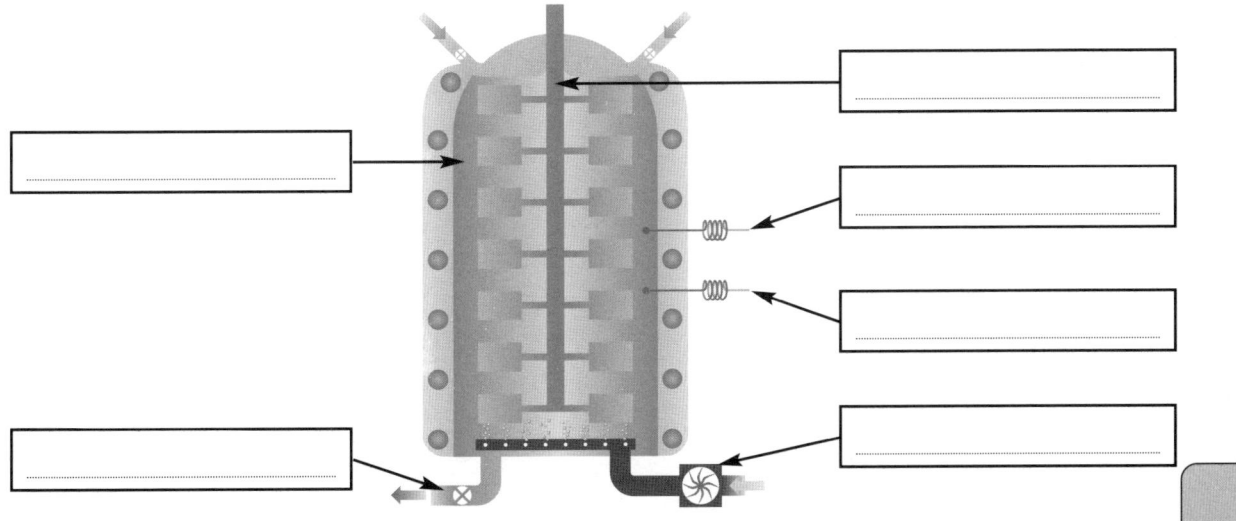

Agriculture and Food

1 Give three reasons why food products are tested during development.

a) _____

b) _____

c) _____

2 a) Which type of test relies on the training of the tester to observe characteristics or deficiencies in food products?

_____

b) Give one disadvantage of this kind of test.

_____

c) Give two examples of this type of test.

i) _____

ii) _____

3 What is the difference between a semi-quantitative and a quantitative test?

_____

_____

4 Give two examples of a semi-quantitative test.

a) _____

b) _____

5 Give two examples of a quantitative test.

a) _____

b) _____

6 Which type of test is the most accurate?

_____

Agriculture and Food

1 What are the two main factors that determine the price of a product?

a) ....

b) ....

2 In which two ways can a government influence the price of products?

a) ....

b) ....

3 a) Explain the importance of advertising for a product.

....

....

b) A company is about to launch a new fruit juice. Design a marketing poster to advertise this new product. Include any features, slogans or images that you think are important to bring the product to the attention of the public.

```
┌─────────────────────────────────────────────────────────────┐
│                                                               │
│                                                               │
│                                                               │
│                                                               │
│                                                               │
│                                                               │
│                                                               │
│                                                               │
│                                                               │
│                                                               │
└─────────────────────────────────────────────────────────────┘
```

4 a) Explain why a quality mark on a product adds market value to a product.

....

....

b) Give two examples of quality marks that can be added to a product.

i) ....

ii) ....

Glossary

1 Fill in the crossword below.

Across

3. A specialist in the treatment of skeletal-muscular injuries (15)

5. Tissue which connects a muscle to a bone (6)

9. A farming technique in which the welfare of the animals is considered to be very important (7)

11. Vessels which carry blood from the organs to the heart (5)

12. Vessels which carry blood away from the heart towards the organs (8)

13. A calculation which compares a person's weight to his/her height (3)

14. Vessels that connect arteries to veins (11)

16. A measurement of the number of times a heart beats each minute (5,4)

17. The mass of a product that has had all the water removed (3)

18. Particles found in blood plasma (9)

19. Tissue which connects bones to a joint (8)

Down

1. A form of respiration which uses oxygen (7)

2. A specialised cell formed by meiosis (6)

3. A microorganism that causes disease (8)

4. Can be measured using a liquid crystal thermometer (11)

6. A organism that has had its genetic make-up altered is _____ modified (11)

7. An imaging technique that is used to see if a bone is broken (4)

8. A form of respiration which takes place without oxygen (8)

10. A term used for a breeding programme where animals are deliberately selected for their favourable characteristics (9)

15. A visible effect of a disease or illness (7)

Scientific Detection

1 a) Below is a list of roles carried out by people with scientific expertise. Arrange them in the table below according to whether you would expect them to be employed in **law enforcement**, **environmental protection** or **consumer protection**.

Trading standards officer	Crime scene investigator	Environmental protection officer
Forensic scientist	Food safety officer	Forensic imaging specialist
Ecological appraisal officer	Public analyst	Field monitoring and data officer

Law Enforcement	Environmental Protection	Consumer Protection

b) Choose one of the jobs listed above and write a brief summary of what the role involves. You can use the Internet or another secondary source to help you.

....

....

....

....

2 a) List three other industries that need to employ scientific experts in different roles.

i) ....

ii) ....

iii) ....

b) Suggest two reasons why it is essential that only specially trained experts work in these roles.

i) ....

ii) ....

Scientific Detection

3 Think about the different services provided by the Forensic Science Service, Environment Agency and Food Standards Agency.

a) Which organisation might a home buyer contact if he/she wanted to find out about flood risk, landfill sites and industrial discharges in the area surrounding the house he/she wants to buy?

_____

b) Which organisation might a lawyer contact if he/she wanted a paternity test carrying out for one of his/her clients?

_____

c) Which organisation is responsible for monitoring the quality of tap water? _____

d) Which organisation might you contact for advice on food allergies? _____

4 Explain why it is essential that the scientific data collected by organisations is accurate and reliable.

_____

_____

_____

5 In general terms, what does it mean if an organisation is **accredited**?

_____

_____

6 Why is it beneficial for these organisations to use standard or common practices when carrying out research and collecting data?

_____

_____

_____

7 What is achieved by carrying out proficiency tests, i.e. where many different laboratories are asked to carry out the same tests on identical samples?

_____

_____

8 Good laboratory practice depends on adherence to health and safety regulations. Name two other factors that constitute good practice.

a) _____

b) _____

Scientific Detection

1 Chromatography is a technique used in scientific detection. In which of the following scenarios would the use of chromatography be appropriate? Place a tick next to the correct answer.

a) To find out the concentration of an acid. ☐

b) To analyse the chemical make-up of a mixture. ☐

c) To produce a DNA profile from a blood sample. ☐

2 Use a line to link each of the following terms, that relate to chromatography, to its correct definition.

Mobile phase	The visual output of chromatography
Stationary phase	The solvent used to move the solution
Chromatogram	The medium that the solvent passes through

3 A customs officer finds a bag of white powder when searching through a traveller's rucksack. The traveller tells him it is washing powder. The substance is sent to a forensic laboratory so that it can be analysed using chromatography. The results are shown below.

white powder | cocaine | heroin | detergent ← origin
known chemicals

a) Why were samples of cocaine, heroin and detergent also tested?

....

....

b) What substance is the white powder?

....

Scientific Detection

3 (Continued)

c) The forensic scientists used a thin layer chromatography technique. Why do you think they used TLC rather than paper chromatography?

....

d) The substances on the resulting chromatogram were all colourless. Describe one method that the forensic scientists might have used to view the chromatogram.

....

....

4 a) Put a circle around each of the words below that could be used to describe the mobile phase in gas–liquid chromatography.

Liquid   **Gas**   **Reactive**   **Carrier**   **Inert**   **Solid**   **Stationary**

b) Describe, in as much detail as you can, what makes up the stationary phase in gas–liquid chromatography.

....

5 Name one advantage that gas–liquid chromatography has over paper and thin layer chromatography.

....

6 Name one use of gas chromatography.

7 Place a tick in the box next to the statement that best describes how gas–liquid chromatography separates the components in a mixture.

a) The components can be separated because they have different boiling points. ☐

b) The components can be separated because they have different solubilities. ☐

c) The components can be separated because they have different molecular masses. ☐

8 Briefly explain what tables of relative retention times show.

1 a) Name one use of DNA profiling.

b) DNA profiles can be obtained from small biological samples. Apart from blood, name two substances that could potentially provide DNA for profiling.

i) ....

ii) ....

HT

2 Explain, in as much detail as possible, how electrophoresis separates components in a mixture.

3 Colour in the two strips of litmus paper to show what colour they become when placed in…

a) an alkali solution

b) an acid solution.

4 a) How does a test using universal indicator paper compare to a test using litmus paper? Mention one similarity and one difference.

b) Write **quantitative** or **qualitative** alongside each of these definitions, as appropriate.

i) Data that provides a measure of quantity or amount. ....

ii) Information that allows the identification of kind or type. ....

c) Explain why the results obtained from using universal indicator solution are described as semi-quantitative.

5 a) Name two common uses of colour test kits in medical diagnosis.

i) ....   ii) ....

b) For the uses you have named above, what bodily fluid is tested with the colour test kits?

Scientific Detection

1 A colorimeter can be used to find the concentration of a coloured solution.

a) Does a colorimeter produce qualitative or quantitative results?

....

b) What does a colorimeter measure? ....

c) What does the reading taken from a colorimeter represent?

....

d) Number the following stages 1 to 5, to show the sequence of events that are followed when carrying out a test using a colorimeter.

    i) Plot the data for the standard solutions to produce a calibration graph. ☐

    ii) Pass light through a pure, colourless solvent and set the colorimeter to zero. ☐

    iii) Test the solution of unknown concentration. ☐

    iv) Use the calibration graph to determine its concentration. ☐

    v) Prepare and test standard solutions using the same solvent. ☐

e) What is a standard solution? ....

2 Six standard glucose solutions of various concentrations are prepared. Benedict's solution is added to the standard solutions. Benedict's solution is blue. It turns red in the presence of glucose. The results are shown below.

Concentration (mg/cm³)	0	0.03	0.06	0.09	0.12	0.15
Absorbance	0	0.045	0.150	0.255	0.360	0.465

a) Use these results to plot a calibration graph on the graph paper provided.

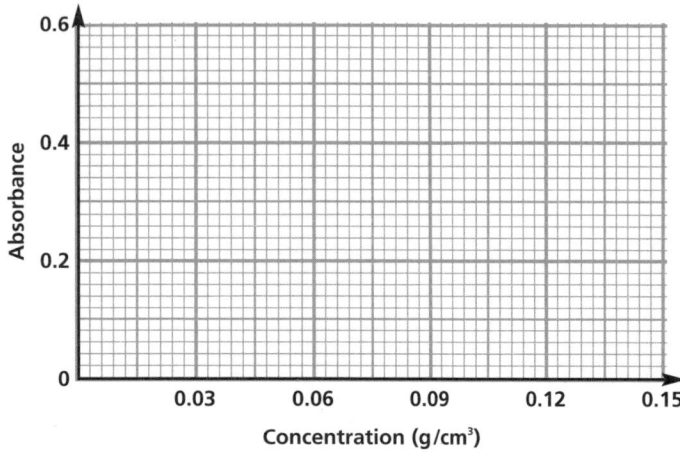

b) Three glucose solutions of unknown concentrations are tested using the colorimeter, and give the readings shown in the table. Complete the table, using your calibration graph to find the concentrations of solutions A, B and C.

Solution	Absorbance	Concentration (mg/cm³)
A	0.170	**i)**
B	0.02	**ii)**
C	0.400	**iii)**

3 Forensic scientists collect a number of samples at a crime scene, which need to be analysed. For each sample suggest the most appropriate testing method.

a) A mud sample, which needs the different components, and their relative amounts, to be identified to find out where it has come from.

b) Testing a colourless liquid in a plastic bottle to find out if it is acidic.

4 Unscramble the anagrams to find four different ways in which detectives can start to build up an image of a crime suspect. For each example, write down where or how they might obtain it.

a) DICEINSPORT

b) TRAPHOGHOP

c) DOVIE

d) DARNWIG

5 a) Take a linear measurement of the following lengths.

i) ————————————— ii) iii)

b) Calculate the area of the following shape.

HT **7** Explain, in as much detail as possible, what a Vernier scale is and how it is used.

Scientific Detection

1 Using the words provided, label the diagram of the compound light microscope below.

Objective lens   **Eyepiece**   **Light source**   **Coarse focus**   **Fine focus**   **Stage**

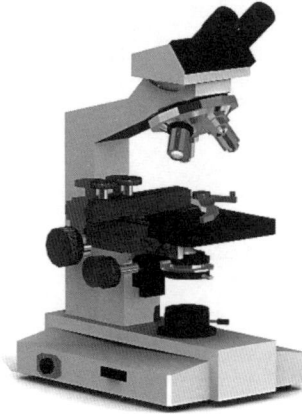

2 A student is preparing a slide of cells from an onion, to study under a light microscope.

a) Use the words below to fill in the gaps and complete the instructions for preparing the slide. You can use the same word more than once.

cover slip   air   tweezers   blotting   stain   onion   slide   water

1. Take a small piece of .... and, using .... , carefully peel off

   the thin, tissue-like membrane from the underside.

2. Lay the membrane flat on the surface of a clean glass .... and add one drop of

   ....

3. Using a mounted .... , lower a thin glass .... over the

   membrane being careful not to trap any .... bubbles.

4. Place a drop of coloured .... at the edge of the ....

5. Draw the .... under the .... by using a piece of

   .... paper to remove the ....

b) The student places the slide on the stage of the microscope. In which order should she use the two focus controls to bring the cells into focus?

   ....

c) The student finds that at x10 she can clearly see the structure of each cell. If the eyepiece lens has a magnification of x8, calculate the total magnifying power used. Show your working.

   ....

HT

3 **a)** What is meant by the term **resolving power**?

_____

_____

b) What limits the resolving power of light microscopes?

_____

4 _A light microscope has a very shallow depth of field._ Explain this statement.

_____

_____

5 **a)** In terms of the structure of an atom, describe an electron.

_____

_____

b) Place a tick beside the statement that best describes the difference between a light microscope and an electron microscope.

i) An electron microscope is so powerful, you can see the electrons of an atom through it. ☐

ii) An electron microscope uses electricity to change the properties of light. ☐

iii) An electron microscope uses a beam of electrons instead of light. ☐

6 Would you use a light microscope or an electron microscope to look at a living spider? Explain your answer.

_____

_____

7 List two advantages of using light microscopes compared to electron microscopes.

a) _____

b) _____

Harnessing Chemicals

1 a) Draw lines between the boxes to show whether each description relates to **organic** or **inorganic** chemicals.

Obtained from sources that have never lived

Chemicals which are extracted from rocks and ores

Compounds which contain carbon

Can be obtained from living or non-living sources

Organic

Inorganic

b) Name two substances obtained from living sources.

i) .... **ii)** ....

c) Name two substances obtained from non-living sources.

i) .... **ii)** ....

d) Name two substances obtained from sources that have never lived.

i) .... **ii)** ....

e) Explain where non-living sources are derived from.

....

....

2 a) The chemical industry refers to the production of **bulk** chemicals and **fine** chemicals. What is the difference between these two types of chemicals?

....

b) Unscramble the anagrams to find four chemicals that are produced in bulk.

i) CHIPSHOPOR AIDC .... **ii)** CURLUSIF CIDA ....

iii) MAMAION .... **iv)** DUOISM DRYHIDEOX ....

c) Choose one of the bulk chemicals from part **b)** and describe one way in which it is used.

....

d) Name one type of fine chemical. ....

3 a) Which company is responsible for regulating health and safety risks during the extraction, manufacture and use of chemicals in the UK?

....

b) Sketch the symbol that would be found on a package containing…

i) a toxic chemical

ii) a corrosive chemical

iii) a highly flammable chemical.

4 a) Identify and label the following items of laboratory equipment:

....

b) Name four items which could be used for measuring out and transferring chemicals.

i) ....   **ii)** ....

iii) ....   **iv)** ....

c) Name two items that could be used as containers for chemical reactions.

i) ....   **ii)** ....

d) Name four items that could be used to increase the temperature conditions of a reaction.

i) ....   **ii)** ....

iii) ....   **iv)** ....

Harnessing Chemicals

1 a) Without looking at the periodic table, write down the symbols for the following chemicals.

    i) Carbon.................................... **ii)** Zinc................................... **iii)** Nitrogen...................

    iv) Hydrogen............................ **v)** Chlorine.......................... **vi)** Oxygen.....................

b) For each symbol given below, write down the name of the chemical it represents.

    i) Ca .... **ii)** Mg ....

    iii) K .... **iv)** Na ....

2 Complete the table below, identifying the different elements in each compound and the ratio of their atoms. The first one has been done for you.

Formula	Elements	Ratio of Atoms for Different Elements
CO_2	Carbon, Oxygen	1:2
H_2O		2:1
CaO	Calcium, Oxygen	
$NaOH$		
$ZnCO_3$		
Na_2CO_3		
$Ca(OH)_2$		1:2:2
$Mg(OH)_2$		

HT

3 a) Write down the relative atomic mass (A_r) for each of the elements given below. You can use the periodic table at the back of this book to help you.

    i) Mg .... **ii)** C .... **iii)** O .... **iv)** S .... **v)** Ca ....

b) Calculate the relative formula mass for each of the compounds given below. Show your working.

    i) $MgCO_3$ ....

    ii) $MgSO_4$ ....

    iii) $CaCO_3$ ....

HT

1 Complete the table showing the names and formulae for oxides, hydroxides and salts.

Compound	Formula
calcium carbonate	a)
sodium sulfate	b)
calcium oxide	c)
potassium nitrate	d)
e)	KCl
f)	$Mg(OH)_2$
g)	Na_2CO_3
h)	$CaCl_2$
zinc oxide	i)
j)	$MgSO_4$

2 a) Write down the chemical formulae for the following acids:

i) hydrochloric acid .... **ii)** sulfuric acid ....

iii) nitric acid ....

b) Looking at their formulae, what do all these acids have in common?

....

3 Use the words provided to complete the word equations below. You may need to use some of the words more than once.

water   salt   oxide   carbonate

i) acid + metal ⟶ .... + hydrogen

ii) acid + metal .... ⟶ .... + water

iii) acid + metal hydroxide ⟶ .... + ...

iv) acid + metal .... ⟶ .... + ... + carbon dioxide

Harnessing Chemicals

4 A few drops of universal indicator solution are added to acid in a beaker. The acid turns red. An alkali is then gradually added to the acid until the universal indicator turns green.

a) What type of reaction has taken place?

_____

b) What type of substance will have been formed as a result of this reaction?

_____

c) What is the pH of this substance?

_____

5 Solve the clues to complete the crossword below.

Across

6. The mixture formed when a substance is dissolved in a liquid (8)

8. A substance with a pH lower than 7 (4)

9. A liquid in which 7 down can be dissolved (7)

10. Able to dissolve (7)

Down

1. Used to describe a substance that will not dissolve (9)

2. A type of 6 across; formed when a substance is dissolved in water (7)

3. A type of 6 across; formed when a substance is dissolved in a liquid other than water (10)

4. A method used to separate solid particles from a liquid by passing the mixture through a permeable material (10)

5. A solid which comes out of 6 across during a reaction (11)

7. A solid substance that can be dissolved (6)

Harnessing Chemicals

1 a) Each of the statements below describes one of the steps used in the procedure for making an insoluble salt by mixing two solutions.

Number the steps 1 to 5 to show the correct order.

i) Combine the two solutions and stir to mix. ☐

ii) Ensure that all traces of the chemicals are removed from the container and included in the filtration. ☐

iii) Measure out known volumes of two solutions into separate measuring beakers. ☐

iv) Dry out the insoluble salt. ☐

v) Separate the resulting precipitate from the solution by filtration. ☐

b) This diagram shows the two different substances collected at the end of this procedure. Clearly label the **filtrate** and the **insoluble residue**.

c) Name two insoluble chemicals that can be made by reacting two solutions in this way and, for each one, write a word equation to show the reaction that takes place.

i) ....

ii) ....

d) Give the symbol equation for each of the word equations you have written in part **c)**. Remember to check that they balance and include the state symbols.

i) ....

ii) ....

Harnessing Chemicals

1 a) Use the words below to complete the passage which describes how soluble salts are made using an insoluble chemical and a solution. You may need to use some words more than once.

| **filtrate** | **solution** | **soluble** | **insoluble** | **filtered** | **crystallisation** | **solid** | **reaction** |

A _____ salt can be made by reacting an excess quantity of an _____

chemical with a _____ . The _____ mixture is _____

to remove the excess of the _____ chemical. The _____ product is

then obtained from the _____ by _____ .

b) Put the following words into the flow chart below to show the correct order of the stages used to produce a soluble salt.

Filtration   Crystallisation   Filtration   Evaporation   Wash and Dry   Reaction

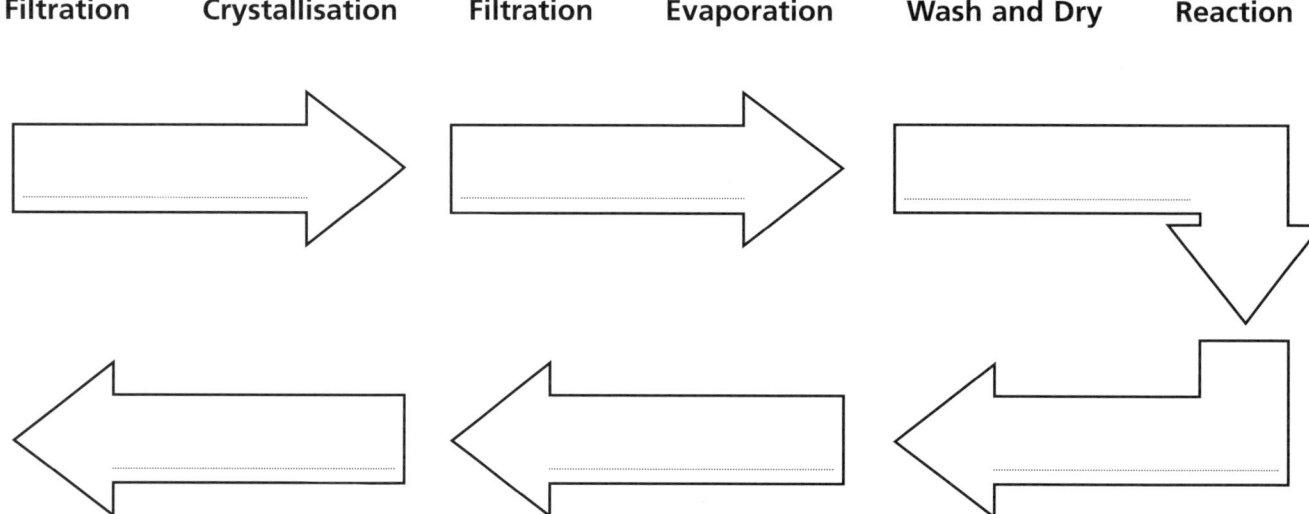

c) Charlotte is making an insoluble salt from a metal hydroxide and acid solution. However, the crystals she produces are very small. Explain how she could obtain larger crystals in a repeat experiment.

_____

_____

2 a) Use the words below to complete the passage which describes how soluble salts are made using two solutions.

| **instant** | **crystallisation** | **solutions** | **salt** | **reactants** | **observe** | **sufficient** |

A soluble _____ can be made by reacting two _____ .

The solid is produced by _____ . The reactions are _____ .

It is important to _____ the reaction, to make sure that _____

amounts of the _____ have been used.

b) A soluble salt is formed in this way when an acid is neutralised with an alkali.

   i) What is the name of the method used in laboratories to carry out and monitor neutralisation reactions?

   ii) Name a chemical indicator that can be used to monitor neutralisation reactions, and explain how it can be used to see when the reaction is complete.

   iii) Write a word equation for one example of a neutralisation reaction.

   HT   **iv)** Write the balanced symbol equation for the word equation you have written above. Make sure that you include state symbols.

3 a) Look at the following compounds and their formulae. What do they have in common?
CH_4 (methane), C_2H_6 (ethane), C_3H_6 (propene) and C_4H_8 (butene).

b) CH_3OH (methanol), C_2H_5OH (ethanol) and C_3H_7OH (propanol) are all alcohols. Looking at their formulae, what does this functional group have in common?

c) CH_3CO_2H (ethanoic acid) and $C_2H_5CO_2H$ (propanoic acid) are carboxylic acids. Looking at their formulae, what does this functional group have in common?

4 Draw the displayed formula for CH_4 (methane).

Harnessing Chemicals

5 a) Sort each of the chemical formulae provided below into the correct group in the table – **hydrocarbon, alcohol** or **carboxylic acid**.

$C_5H_{11}OH$ $CH_3(CH_2)_{10}CO_2H$ $C_{10}H_{20}$ $CH_3CH_2CH_2CO_2H$

$C_{20}H_{22}$ $C_8H_{17}OH$ $C_{10}H_{21}OH$ $C_6H_5CO_2H$ $C_{15}H_{30}$

Hydrocarbon	Alcohol	Carboxylic Acid

b) i) Which type of chemical has the functional group **-C-OH**? ....

ii) Which type of chemical has the functional group **-CO₂H** (or **COOH**)? ....

6 a) Write a brief definition for each of the following words.

i) Distillation: ....

....

ii) Reflux: ....

....

iii) Distillate: ....

....

b) Use all three words from part **a)** to describe how esters are formed.

....

....

HT

c) Write the word equation for the reaction by which an ester is formed.

....

Harnessing Chemicals

1 What is meant by the term **rate of reaction**?

....

....

2 List three methods used for following the rate of a chemical reaction.

a) ....

b) ....

c) ....

3 a) Which three factors affect the rate of a chemical reaction?

i) ....

ii) ....

iii) ....

HT **b) i)** *Reducing the temperature of the reaction mixture increases the rate of reaction.*
Is this statement **true** or **false**? Explain your answer in as much detail as possible.

....

....

ii) *Breaking up a lump of an insoluble solid into smaller particles will slow down the rate of reaction.*
Is this statement **true** or **false**? Explain your answer in as much detail as possible.

....

....

iii) *Increasing the concentration of a solution will increase the rate of reaction.*
Is this statement **true** or **false**? Explain your answer in as much detail as possible.

....

....

....

Harnessing Chemicals

1 The production of bulk chemicals is very costly.

a) Suggest four things that a commercial chemical manufacturer would have to spend money on.

i) .... ii) ....

iii) .... iv) ....

b) Conserving energy can help to reduce bulk chemical production costs.

i) Suggest one other advantage of conserving energy.

....

....

ii) Suggest one method of conserving energy in bulk chemical production.

....

2 a) Explain the difference between an exothermic reaction and an endothermic reaction.

....

b) Suggest one way in which energy can be conserved when an exothermic reaction takes place.

....

3 Pure iron can be extracted from an ore called haematite (Fe_2O_3). An industrial plant manager calculates that 3500 tonnes of iron can be extracted from 5000 tonnes of Fe_2O_3. In practice, only 3100 tonnes of iron is obtained from 5000 tonnes of Fe_2O_3.

a) Calculate the percentage yield. (Show all your working.)

....

....

HT **b)** The industrial plant manager calculated that 3500 tonnes of iron could be obtained from 5000 tonnes of Fe_2O_3. Is this an accurate theoretical yield? Explain your answer, showing all your working.

....

....

Harnessing Chemicals

1 There are three main grades of chemical purity: **laboratory grade**, **technical grade** and **analytical grade**.

a) Write down the three grades in order of purity, starting with the purest.

_____

b) Write down the three grades in order of relative cost, starting with the cheapest.

_____

c) What grade of chemicals would be used…

i) to produce a new drug for treating cancer? _____

ii) by researchers in the preliminary stages of developing a new product? _____

iii) in a chemical plant which manufactures bulk chemicals for commercial use? _____

2 A research scientist develops a new chemical that will be useful in the manufacture of certain products. List four factors that will need to be considered when planning the best way to produce the chemical on an industrial scale.

a) _____ **b)** _____

c) _____ **d)** _____

HT

3 Complete the table below, comparing batch process and continuous process chemical production.

Type of Process	Brief Description	Advantages	Disadvantages
Batch			
Continuous			

Harnessing Chemicals

1 **a)** With reference to chemical processes, what does the term **sustainable** mean?

....

....

b) List the four key features of a fully sustainable chemical process.

i) ....

ii) ....

iii) ....

iv) ....

2 Alloys and emulsions are two different types of mixtures.

a) What is the difference between a chemical mixture and a chemical compound?

....

b) Name two common products that are emulsions.

....

c) Some foods, like low-fat spreads and mayonnaise, have emulsifying agents added to them. What does the emulsifying agent do?

....

d) What is an alloy?

....

e) Suggest two alloys, and one practical use for each.

i) Alloy: ....

Use: ....

ii) Alloy: ....

Use: ....

3 List three key reasons why it is important for the chemical production in chemical plants to be subject to a quality control process.

a) ....

b) ....

c) ....

4 A 100cm³ copper sulfate solution is made using 10g copper sulfate to a concentration of 0.1g/cm³. Describe the stages involved in mixing the formula to the specified concentration.

....

....

....

....

....

....

5 Which two measurements can concentration be expressed in?

a) ....

b) ....

6 Calculate the mass of a solute if the concentration of a formulation is 65g/litre and the volume is 22cm³. Show your workings.

....

....

....

HT **7** What other measurement can concentration be measured in?

....

Glossary

1 Fill in the missing words in the definitions below, and then find them in the wordsearch.

a) _____ chemicals are produced on a large scale.

b) An _____ reaction gives out energy to the surroundings.

c) A _____ microscope can be used to view living organisms.

d) In paper chromatography, the _____ is

the solvent that carries the chemicals through the stationary phase.

e) The reaction between an acid and a base which forms a neutral solution is called

_____ .

f) An _____ is a substance that contains one liquid finely dispersed within

another one.

g) The amount of product that is obtained from a reaction is called the _____ .

h) An_____ solution is made when a solute dissolves in water.

N	A	V	B	A	S	N	S	W	P	B	Y	K
E	J	O	D	U	U	S	C	O	E	Q	G	R
U	M	O	B	I	L	E	P	H	A	S	E	O
T	R	R	J	Z	I	K	P	E	M	W	B	T
R	E	X	O	T	H	E	R	M	I	C	I	U
A	P	A	Y	C	Y	J	T	N	P	T	D	B
L	X	B	I	F	Q	F	O	B	B	N	I	E
I	J	S	E	M	G	I	T	K	O	X	N	O
S	D	M	L	J	S	D	Q	A	M	R	D	C
A	A	S	D	L	O	M	B	M	S	T	H	N
T	Q	G	U	S	B	H	D	E	W	O	P	T
I	U	M	Q	L	I	G	H	T	O	H	J	C
O	E	Q	U	B	P	J	H	S	R	T	U	I
N	O	E	K	S	V	G	Q	F	P	G	K	F
S	U	P	D	X	A	R	D	K	U	C	O	H
A	S	Y	O	K	B	X	B	N	N	N	T	P
Z	M	H	C	R	W	Z	M	A	F	Y	R	W

1 Connect each component to its correct symbol.

Component Name
Fuse
Loudspeaker
Buzzer
Light dependent resistor
Amplifier
Light emitting diode
Fixed Resistor
Variable resistor
Transformer
Capacitor

Component Symbol
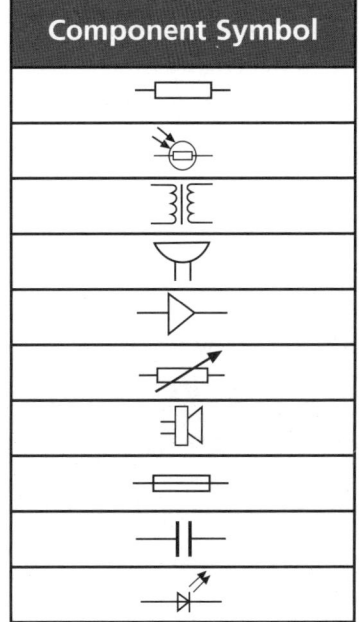

2 A series circuit contains a bulb, a fixed resistor and a 12V battery. If the resistor has a voltage of 8V across it, what is the voltage across the bulb?

HT

3 a) The diagram opposite shows a parallel circuit. Write in the missing ammeter reading.

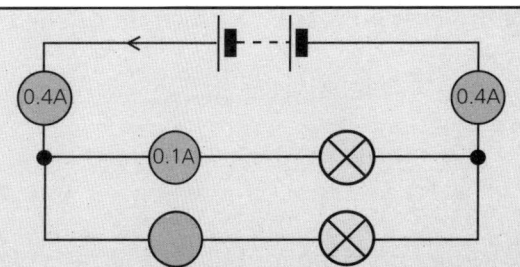

b) The current through each bulb is different. Explain why.

---

c) i) In the space below, draw a parallel circuit with a battery and 2 loudspeakers.

ii) If the current through each loudspeaker is 3A, calculate the current running through the battery.

Communications

1. Write down the formula that links voltage, current and resistance.

   ....

2. Explain what is meant by **resistance**.

   ....

   ....

   ....

3. Complete the table below:

Voltage (Volts)	Current (Amps)	Resistance (Ohms)
12	2	a) ....
6	3	b) ....
c)	4	1.5
d)	0.1	2200
5	e)	5
220	f)	20

4. *Power is a measure of the rate of energy transfer.* Explain what is meant by this statement.

   ....

   ....

   ....

5. Write down the formula used to calculate power. ....

6. Calculate the heating power of an electric heater that has a current of 10A and a supply voltage of 200V.

   ....

   ....

7. What would be the voltage of a travel iron that has a power output of 1320W when running at 12A?

   ....

   ....

HT 8. Briefly explain how electronic circuits are designed to stop too large a current damaging the components.

   ....

9. Explain in what situation it would be preferable to use batteries to provide power for a communications device.

   ....

1 Draw a block diagram to show the three stages of a basic communications system.

2 Briefly explain what function the following devices have in an electronic system.

  a) Input devices: _____

  b) Output devices: _____

3 a) Give an example of a communications system that uses microwaves.

  _____

  b) Draw a block diagram naming the three stages of your system.

  c) Describe what the processor stage does in your example.

  _____

  _____

4 Why are block diagrams used?

  _____

5 Give an example of a simple signalling system, explaining what the function is at each stage.

Input: _____   Function: _____

Processor: _____   Function: _____

Output: _____   Function: _____

Communications

1 Complete the following sentences.

A signal which can have any value is called .... Examples of this type of

signal are .... and .... A signal which is

transmitted as a series of ones and .... is called ....

2 a) Give two advantages of sending analogue signals.

  i) ....

  ii) ....

b) Give two disadvantages of sending analogue signals.

  i) ....

  ii) ....

3 a) Give two advantages of sending digital signals.

  i) ....

  ii) ....

b) Give two disadvantages of sending digital signals.

  i) ....

  ii) ....

HT **4 a)** Explain what is meant by the term **signal-to-noise ratio**.

  ....

  ....

b) Does a digital signal have a **high** or **low** signal-to-noise ratio? Explain your answer.

  ....

  ....

1 Write a definition for each of the following terms:

a) **A bit:** ....

b) **A byte:** ....

c) **A word:** ....

2 When converting from an analogue signal to a digital signal, the analogue signal is sampled. Explain what is meant by the **sample rate**.

....

....

....

3 Name two problems that can occur with a low sample rate.

a) ....

b) ....

4 Explain why a high sample rate requires a large amount of data to be sent.

....

....

....

5 A music signal is sampled at a very high sample rate using a large number of bits per word. This has the disadvantage of producing a high bit rate and, therefore, requires a large amount of data to be sent. Explain why, despite this, a high sample rate is used.

....

....

HT **6** How can compression help to reduce the problem of slow transmission speeds?

....

....

....

Communications

1 a) Give three link types which can be used for transmitting electrical signals from place to place.

i) ....

ii) ....

iii) ....

b) A communication design engineer is deciding what link type to use for communication across a high-speed computer network. What type of link do you think should be used? Explain your answer.

....

....

....

....

2 a) The following blocks describe how information is passed from one fax machine to another; they are in the wrong order. Number them 1 to 5 to put them into the correct order.

Long distance link	Local exchange	Fax machine	Local exchange	Fax machine

....

b) For each of the following blocks, state whether the signal is likely to be analogue or digital.

i) Local exchange: ....

ii) Fax machine: ....

iii) Long distance link: ....

3 State three devices which can store electronic information.

a) ....

b) ....

c) ....

4 Match each of the following key terms to its definition.

Encode	The distance over which information can be sent
Decode	To put information into a code
Range	The number of pictures per second that make up a video
Pixel	The amount of information sent per second
Refresh rate	To extract the information from a code
Data transmission rate	A single point on an image

5 Semaphore is a code based on using flags at different positions to represent letters. Anil and Clare are standing at either end of a netball court. Anil is sending a short message to Clare using Semaphore. Using the words **encodes**, **range** and **decodes**, explain how the message is being sent from Anil to Clare.

_____

_____

_____

_____

6 Video data sent over the Internet is normally of lower quality than television broadcasts. Explain why.

_____

_____

_____

7 Give two examples of ways in which the **distance** of human communication has increased in recent years.

a) _____

b) _____

8 Suggest one recent invention that has caused a huge increase in the **quality** of information that is sent and received.

_____

Communications

9 Give two examples of ways in which the **quantity** of communication has increased.

a) .... **b)** ....

10 a) Explain, in as much detail as you can, how radio waves are sent and received. Include the words **signal**, **carrier wave** and **modulated** in your answer.

....

....

....

....

b) Explain why an amplifier might be used.

....

HT **11 a)** A radio wave can be modulated in two different ways. Describe the difference between the two types of modulated wave.

....

....

....

....

b) Sketch a diagram for each type of wave to help explain your answer to part **a)**.

Frequency Modulation

Voltage | Time

Amplitude Modulation

Voltage | Time

Communications

1 Complete the following sentences:

Radio waves can be _____ and _____ by obstructions and the

atmosphere. Different waves are reflected and absorbed by _____ amounts. Therefore,

the _____ of a wave determines how it can be used in a _____ system.

2 Match each type of aerial up to its use and other details.

Aerial Type
Simple dipole
Ferrite rod
Dish receiver

Use
Mobile phone
Walkie-talkie
Satellite television

Other Details
Needs to point in correct direction
Makes signal stronger
Has 360° reception

3 a) Suggest one cause of interference in radio waves.

_____

b) Why is interference undesirable?

_____

c) Suggest one way in which interference can be reduced.

_____

4 Briefly outline one of the roles of Ofcom and explain why its work is necessary.

_____

_____

_____

_____

_____

Communications

1 **a)** Write down the formula used to calculate wave speed.

_____

b) Given that all radio waves travel at the same speed, what does the formula tell us about how the frequency and wavelength are related?

_____

_____

2 A radio wave travels at 300 000 000m/s, with a wavelength of 50m. Calculate the frequency of the wave.

_____

_____

3 A radio wave travels at 300 000 000m/s, with a frequency of 800 000Hz. Calculate the wavelength.

_____

_____

4 **a)** Briefly explain what diffraction is, in terms of radio waves.

_____

b) When is diffraction most obvious?

_____

c) Sketch a diagram to show what happens to radio waves when they pass through a gap much smaller than the wavelength.

1 The following questions are about the production of an outdoor news broadcast.

a) Who is responsible for ensuring the balance in the volume of music, background noise and different people's voices? (Circle the correct answer.)

       Editor   **Sound engineer**   **Camera crew**   **reporter**

b) State the job title of the person who would be responsible for post-production editing.

....

c) What role would an orbital satellite play in the broadcast?

....

....

2 A wireless communications system can be represented with the following blocks.

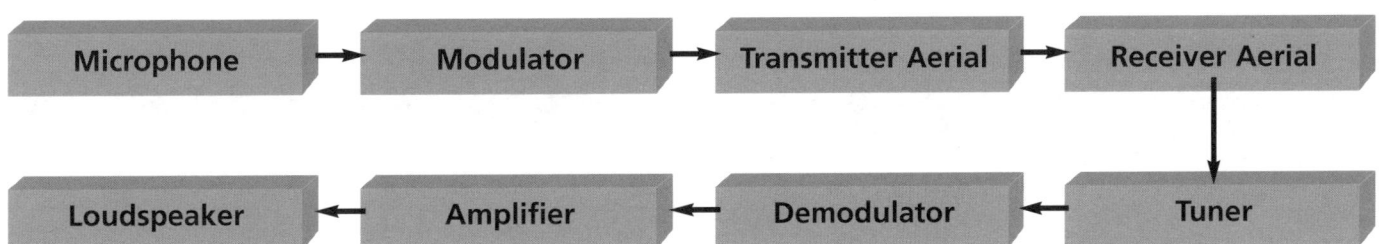

For the following statements, write down which block the statement is referring to.

a) Transmits the carrier and signal as an electromagnetic wave. ....

b) Decodes the signal from the wave to give an electrical signal. ....

c) Encodes the signal onto a carrier wave. ....

d) Increases the amplitude of the electrical signal. ....

e) Converts the electrical signal into sound. ....

f) Picks up the sound and converts it into an electrical signal. ....

Communications

1 Network coverage is one technical consideration of a communications system. State three other technical issues that companies must consider when deciding on a product specification.

a) ....

b) ....

c) ....

2 Suggest two non-technical issues that companies must also consider when deciding on a new product design.

a) ....

b) ....

3 A company is opening up a new office building for 300 members of staff. They are deciding what type of internal system to use for staff communication. The advantages and disadvantages of three systems are included in the table below:

Mobile Phones	Wireless Radio	PABX Phone System
• Standard phones	• Specialised radios	• Standard phones
• Portable	• Portable	• Not portable
• Battery powered	• Battery operated	• Mains power
• Require charging	• Require charging	• Require installation of automated switchboard
• Can be used for external calls	• Cannot be used for external calls	• Can be used for external calls
• Secure calls	• Other users can pick up private calls	• Secure calls
• Calls are expensive	• Free calls	• Free internal calls

a) Which option would you choose for the office to use?

....

b) Explain your answer to part **a)**.

....

....

....

© Lonsdale

1 In the space below, draw a diagram showing an input block under test.

2 How can the measured voltage be used by a test engineer to indicate if something is wrong?

....

....

3 The diagram opposite shows an oscilloscope trace.

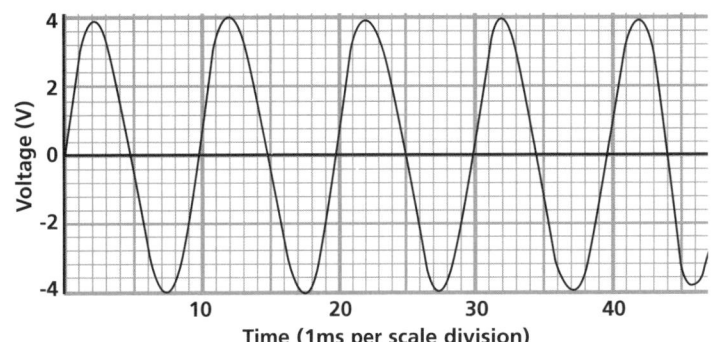

Time (1ms per scale division)

a) What is the amplitude of the signal?

....

b) How long does it take for a complete wave?

....

c) Calculate the frequency (number of waves per second) of the signal.

....

4 On the graph paper, sketch an oscilloscope trace showing a wave that takes 5m/s for each complete wave and has an amplitude of 2 volts.

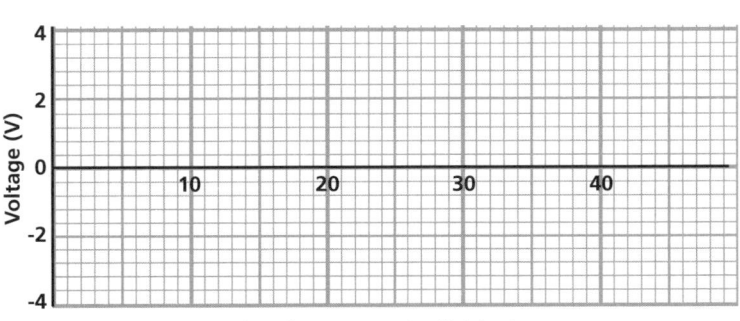

Time (1ms per scale division)

5 On the graph paper, sketch an oscilloscope trace of a wave with an amplitude of 3 volts and a frequency of 500Hz.

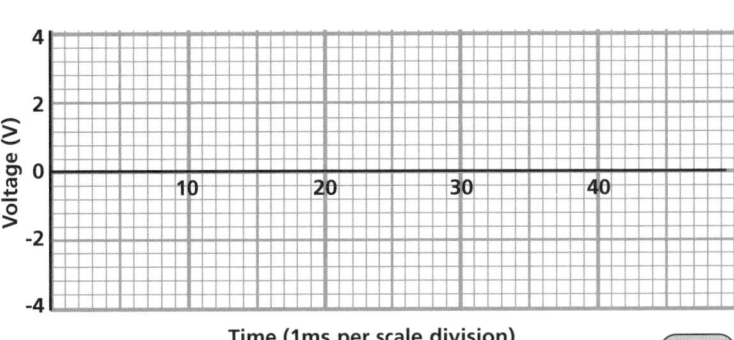

Time (1ms per scale division)

Communications

1 Name an organisation that is responsible for ensuring that electrical equipment is safe to use.

....

2 What do each of the following safety symbols mean?

a) .... b) ....

c) .... d) ....

3 Sketch the safety symbol that is used to show a first aid point.

4 For the following situations, suggest what electrical hazards may be involved and how these hazards could be reduced.

a) Mowing the lawn.   Hazard: ....

How hazard is reduced: ....

b) Drilling a hole in a wall.   Hazard: ....

How hazard is reduced: ....

c) Setting up garden lights. Hazard: ....

How hazard is reduced: ....

5 a) Electrical equipment is fitted with a range of safety features. List two examples.

i) ....

ii) ....

b) Choose one of the safety features in part **a)** and describe how it helps to improve safety.

....

....

Materials and Performance

1 A person who works in industry, research and standards needs to have a good knowledge of materials and their properties.

a) Give one example of such a person.

_____

b) What do you think would be the consequence of the person you named in your answer to part **a)** having a poor knowledge of materials?

_____

2 Complete the table below

Class of Material	Examples	Properties
Metals and Alloys	**a)** _____	**b)** _____
c) _____	Polyethene, polystyrene, polyethylene	**d)** _____
Ceramics	**e)** _____	**f)** _____
g) _____	Oak, chipboard, MDF	Thermal insulators
Composites	**h)** _____	Various, depending on design requirements

3 The British Standards Institution monitors product standards for quality, safety and consistency.

a) Name two other organisations that are responsible for monitoring standards.

i) _____

ii) _____

b) Choose one of the organisations listed in your answer above, and give an example of the type of work carried out by this organisation.

_____

_____

4 Which organisations use the following symbols?

a)  _____

b)  _____

Materials and Performance

1 Using the words below to help you, identify the correct definition for the following explanations.

Stiffness	Toughness	Density	Tensile strength
Hardness	Elastic	Plastic	Compressive strength

a) Describes how resistant a material is to snapping or shattering.

b) Describes how resistant a material is to scratching.

c) Describes how resistant a material is to bending.

d) Describes the maximum force a material can withstand before fracturing.

e) Describes how heavy a material is in relation to its size.

f) Describes a material that will return back to its original shape
when the force on it has been removed.

g) Describes the maximum stretching force needed to break a material.

h) Describes a material that is permanently deformed and will not
return to its original shape.

2 a) Give an example of a material or product that shows high tensile properties.

b) Give an example of a material that is very brittle.

HT

3 A strip of steel is heated. Explain in what way the heat will affect the stiffness of the metal.

4 a) Give an example of an artefact that is designed using materials which have complementary
mechanical properties.

b) Explain how your example given in part **a)** works.

Materials and Performance

1 Explain why an alloy is described as a **solid solution**.

....

....

....

2 Give two examples of composite materials.

a) .... **b)** ....

HT **3** Using a specific example, explain how the materials in a composite can have very useful mechanical properties.

....

....

....

4 A structural engineer was considering using mild steel within the construction of a building, but he has now decided that it will not be strong enough. Suggest three ways in which the strength of the mild steel could be increased.

a) ....

b) ....

c) ....

5 Several different materials are being considered in the design of a new golf club. Their various properties are given below.

	Cost	Durability	Environmental Impact	Performance
Material A	Expensive	Very durable	High	Excellent
Material B	Mid-range price	Very durable	Low	Good
Material C	Cheap	Short lifetime	Low	Average

a) Which material do you think would be the best choice for a mass-produced club aimed at committed amateur golfers? Explain your answer.

....

....

b) Suggest another consideration that may be taken into account when deciding which material to use.

....

Materials and Performance

1 a) Explain the meaning of **electrical conductance**.

....

....

b) In what unit is electrical conductance measured? ....

2 When designing a kettle, which parts should be made out of a material which has a low electrical conductance?

....

....

3 Silver has a higher conductance than copper. Suggest one reason why most electrical wires are made out of copper and not silver.

....

....

HT **4** An electronic circuit was used to test three different materials. The results are shown in the table below.

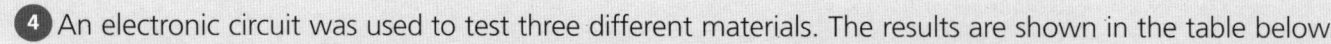

Material 1		Material 2		Material 3	
Voltage	Current	Voltage	Current	Voltage	Current
2	1.8	2	2.2	2	1.5
4	3.9	4	4.3	4	3.0
6	5.5	6	6.7	6	4.4
8	7.0	8	8.8	8	5.9
10	9.0	10	11.0	10	7.7

a) On the graph paper opposite, plot the results for each material and draw a line of best fit for each one.

b) Using your graph, list the materials in order of conductance, starting with the highest.

....

....

....

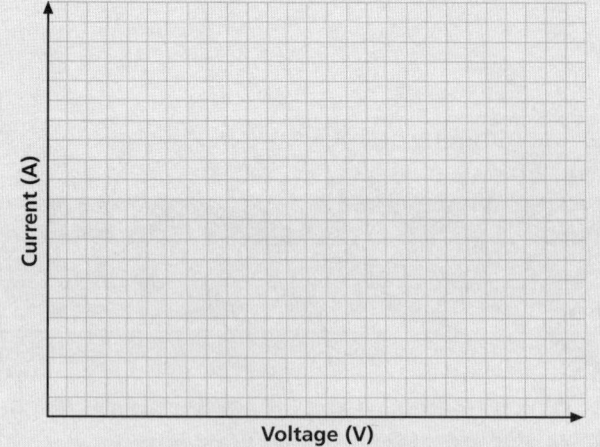

c) i) Write the formula used to calculate conductance.

....

   ii) Calculate the conductance of Material 2.

....

Materials and Performance

1 Explain what is meant by the term **thermal conductance**.

....

2 The picture opposite shows a frying pan.
Label the parts that should have a low thermal
conductance, and the parts that should have
a high thermal conductance.

3 a) Two ice cubes are taken out of a freezer. Ice cube A is placed on a plastic tray and ice cube B is placed
on a metal tray. Which ice cube will melt first? Explain your answer.

....

....

4 Complete the following paragraph using the words below to help you. You may need to use some words
more than once.

| **colder** | **heat** | **slowly** | **conductor** | **copper** | **warmer** |

A substance with a low thermal conductance feels .... than one with a high thermal

conductance. This is because .... flows .... through a poor

.... so when you touch it your hand loses .... slowly. When

holding a good .... e.g. .... your hand loses

.... quickly so the object feels ....

5 The diagram opposite illustrates how thermal expansion
would be measured in a classroom. Explain what
happens as the test material is heated up.

Scale

Sample under test

Pointer

Pin

....

....

....

HT **6** Give an example of a product that is designed using materials which have complementary thermal properties.

....

Materials and Performance

1 The following information describes an experiment in which a material is tested for stiffness.

One end of the test material is clamped on the edge of the bench, with the other end overhanging the bench. A ruler is placed at the overhanging end and different masses are then added to the end. The amount of deflection (bending) that occurs in the material is measured with the ruler.

a) Sketch a diagram for the experiment.

b) A student tests a range of materials with a mass of 100g and obtains the following results:

Material	Deflection 1	Deflection 2	Deflection 3	Average
Cardboard	5.2cm	5.6cm	6cm	
Plywood	3cm	3.4cm	3.2cm	
Aluminium	5cm	6cm	12cm	
Glass	0.2cm	0.1cm	0.2cm	

i) Look at the results and circle any outliers.

ii) Complete the average column in the table.

iii) Which material was the stiffest? ....

iv) Which material was the most flexible? ....

v) Explain whether the evidence is of good enough quality for you to be certain of your answers to parts **iii)** and **iv)**.

....

....

Materials and Performance

2 The diagram opposite illustrates how to test for compressive strength. Write a brief method to explain the procedure.

Weights ⟶

Material

Metal block ⟶

3 Briefly describe how you would test a material for tensile strength.

4 The graph opposite is a force–extension graph.

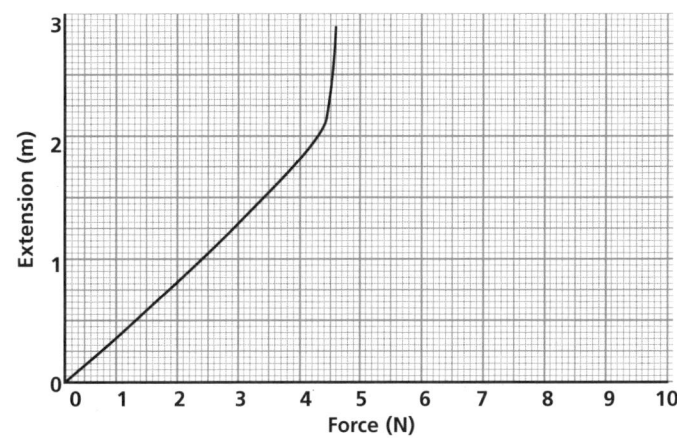

a) Label the elastic limit on the graph.

b) Explain what happens to the material after it has passed the elastic limit.

c) Explain what is meant by the phrase **elastic behaviour**.

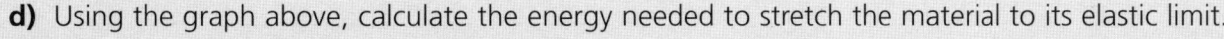

HT

d) Using the graph above, calculate the energy needed to stretch the material to its elastic limit.

5 If a spring has a spring constant of 100N/m, calculate...

a) the force needed to give an extension of 10cm.

b) the energy stored in the spring at this point.

Materials and Performance

1 Are the following statements **true** or **false**?

a) Velocity is the same as speed. ....

b) A resultant force always causes speed to change. ....

c) A resultant force causes a change in velocity. ....

d) If there is no resultant force on an object, the object will move. ....

2 Explain, as fully as you can, how car crumple zones help to increase drivers' safety.

....

....

....

....

3 Give two mechanical properties that a designer would be looking for in a material used to make car seatbelts.

a) ....   **b)** ....

4 The graph opposite shows the force on a car which causes it to accelerate and then reach a constant speed.

a) Use the graph to find the change in momentum.

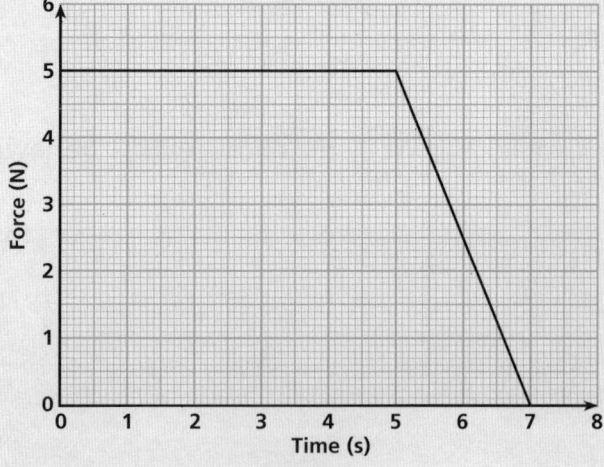

b) Write down the formula that is used to calculate change in momentum.

....

5 a) A car accelerates for 5 seconds with a constant force of 10 000N. Calculate the change in momentum.

....

b) If the car has a mass of 2000kg, what is the increase in velocity?

....

Materials and Performance

1. Use the words below to fill in the gaps in the following sentences. You may need to use each word more than once.

frequency   **sound**   **amplitude**   **pitch**   **decibel**

Whenever an object vibrates it produces .... If the vibrations have a large

.... the sound is louder than vibrations of smaller .... We measure

the loudness of sound on the .... scale.

The number of vibrations per second is called the .... High ....

sounds have a higher .... than low .... sounds.

2. a) The decibel scale is a non-linear scale. Explain what is meant by **non-linear scale**.

....

....

....

b) How many times louder is a 30dB sound than a 10dB sound?

....

....

c) At what decibel level is normal conversation held?

....

....

d) Explain what happens in the human ear at 130dB.

....

....

3. Describe two ways in which sound intensity can be reduced in a building.

a) ....

....

b) ....

....

Materials and Performance

1 Photochromic is a type of specialised glass. Explain what its properties are, and what it is used for.

_____

_____

_____

2 Give two ways in which mirrors, either plane or curved, can be used.

a) _____

b) _____

3 The diagram below shows a convex lens. Complete the diagram showing what happens to the light rays as they hit the lens. The focal length is 3cm. Label the focal length and focal plane.

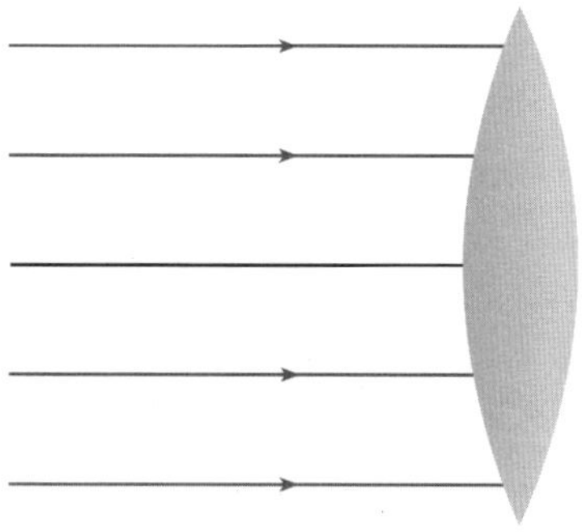

4 Give two factors that can affect the focal length on a lens.

a) _____

b) _____

5 a) Why must contact lenses be un-reactive?

_____

_____

b) Give two other properties that contact lenses need to have.

i) _____

ii) _____

6 Fill in the crossword below.

Across

4. An upside-down image (8)
9. A material which does not let light through (6)
11. A material which lets light pass through it, but clear images cannot be seen through it (11)
12. This happens when light hits a surface and bounces off (10)

Down

1. This happens to light rays as they pass through a concave lens (7)
2. When light changes direction as it passes from one material to another (10)
3. Rays of light passing through this lens are bent inwards (6)
5. An image that cannot be focused on a screen (7)
6. Light passing through this remains coherent (11)
7. A length, a point or a plane (5)
8. An image that is the right way up (7)
10. An image that can be focused on a screen (4)

7 On the diagram below, label the **lens, shutter, focal plane, aperture** and **viewfinder**.

Glossary

1 Fill in the crossword below.

Across

3. The point at which an image is focused (5,5)

6. The speed and direction of an object (8)

8. The number of waves produced within a given time period (9)

12. A signal which can be easily distorted due to interference (8)

13. _____ conductance is a measure of how easily heat flows through an object (7)

14. How high or low a sound is (5)

15. A word used to describe a material that returns to its original shape after a force is removed (7)

16. A signal which uses a fixed range of values (7)

17. A type of lens which causes light rays passing through it to be spread out (9)

18. When a wave front is bent and spreads out as It passes an obstacle or goes through a gap (11)

Down

1. A force which can cause a material to snap (7)

2. The equivalent of eight bits (4)

4. An electric circuit in which there is more than one path for the current to take (8)

5. The percentage of incorrectly transmitted information (5,4)

7. An image which is focused on a screen (4)

9. The name for a force which comprises all the forces acting on an object (9)

10. A force which can cause a material to fracture (11)

11. A material which is comprised of one material embedded within another (9)

Interpreting Information

Agriculture and Food

1 The table below shows how the milk yield from a cow varied with the number of times it was milked per day.

Number of Times the Cow is Milked Per Day	Milk Yield (kg per cow per day)
2	33.6
3	36.7
4	38.6

a) Which number of milkings per day produced the highest milk yield?

....

b) Give one disadvantage with milking a cow this number of times each day. (Hint: think about economic costs.)

....

....

....

2 The following table shows the mass of different apples harvested over a five-week period.

	Week 1 Mass (kg)	Week 2 Mass (kg)	Week 3 Mass (kg)	Week 4 Mass (kg)	Week 5 Mass (kg)	Total Mass (kg)
Golden Delicious	2.3	1.4	1.9	1.1	2.5	
Granny Smith	1.2		0.5	0.8	0.7	4.4
Empire	0.3	1.5	1.9	1.8	2.2	

a) Calculate the crop yield for Granny Smith apples in week 2.

....

b) Calculate the total apple yield for...

i) Golden Delicious .... **ii)** Empire ....

c) Which crop produced the greatest mass?

....

Interpreting Information

Agriculture and Food (cont.)

3 The stages below show what happens in the production of plain white flour:

Stage 1: Stalks are harvested.

Stage 2: Wheat seeds are removed from the stalk.

Stage 3: The seeds are milled (ground up).

Stage 4: Flour is sifted to remove the seed husks.

Stage 5: Flour is bagged and stored in a cool, dry place.

a) Why is the flour stored in a cool, dry environment?

....

b) What would happen if the flour was left in a warm, damp environment?

....

4 An experiment was undertaken to see the effect of temperature on the growth of bacteria. A solution of a food sample was smeared across 3 dishes of agar jelly. The dishes were then sealed and left for 3 days in different temperatures. Dish A was left at -4°C, Dish B at 15°C, and Dish C at 25°C. The results are shown below:

A
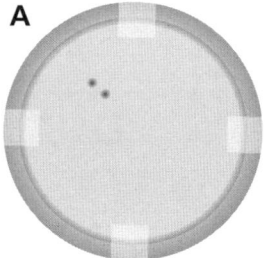

B
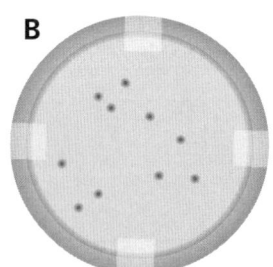

C
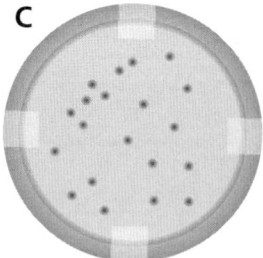

a) How many bacterial colonies have grown in Dish B? ....

b) Which dish has the lowest number of bacterial colonies? ....

c) Which temperature was best for the growth of the bacteria? ....

Interpreting Information

Agriculture and Food (cont.)

5 The stages below show what happens in the brewing of beer:

> **Stage 1:** Water sprinkled onto barley grains.

> **Stage 2:** Grains heated and ground down.

> **Stage 3:** Hops, water and sugar added.

> **Stage 4:** Mixture boiled and left to cool.

> **Stage 5:** Yeast added and fermentation process starts.

> **Stage 6:** Stored in bottles or cans.

a) Why is sugar added to the mixture?

....

b) Why is the mixture boiled?

....

c) Why is the mixture cooled before the yeast is added?

....

HT   **6** The graph below shows the effect of temperature on the photosynthesis of a plant.

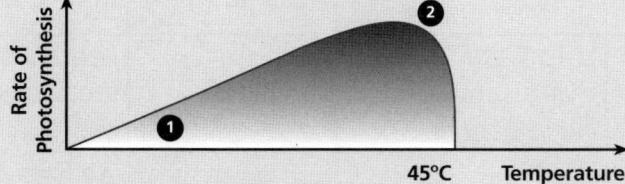

a) The rate of photosynthesis increases at a steady rate from point 1 to point 2. What does this section of the graph show?

....

b) What happens as the temperature approaches 45°C? Explain your answer.

....

....

Interpreting Information

Agriculture and Food (cont.)

1 The incomplete flow chart below shows what happens in the production and processing of chicken and vegetable pies:

> **Stage 1:** Chickens are reared and sent to market.

> **Stage 2:** Chickens sent to slaughterhouse.

> **Stage 3:** Chicken meat cut into pieces. Vegetables added and made into pies.

> **Stage 4:** Pies packaged and stored in freezers.

> **Stage 5:**
> _____

a) Fill in stage 5.

b) Is this an example of a gathered harvest or a whole organism harvest?

_____

2 The table below shows some of the methods that two farmers use on their farms.

	Soil Management	Fertilizers	Water Supply	Wildlife	Energy
Farm A	Use of crop rotation. Soil kept covered. Small fields, separated by hedgerows.	Uses chemical fertilizers and removes weeds with a hoe.	Collects and stores rain water. Manages crops to reduce water loss.	High plant diversity.	Uses non-renewable energy sources and solar power.
Farm B	Large fields, no hedgerows. Same crops grown in fields each year.	Removes weeds with the use of pesticides and nitrates.	Uses water from mains supply. No irrigation system.	Low plant diversity.	Uses all non-renewable energy sources.

a) Explain what is meant by farming in a sustainable way.

_____

b) Does Farm A or Farm B farm in a more sustainable way? Give reasons for your answer.

_____

c) Give two ways in which Farm A does not farm in a sustainable way.

i) _____   **ii)** _____

Scientific Detection

1 The information below gives information about a technique used by the Forensic Science Service.

Since it was first used in the early 1980s, DNA profiling has developed to become more sensitive and more discriminating. In recent years, the Forensic Science Service has developed a new technique that enables scientists to produce DNA profiles from samples containing very few cells. The technique, DNA Low Copy Number (DNA LCN), can be used to investigate a range of serious crimes, especially in cases where standard DNA testing has failed to get a result.

The technique targets areas on items where DNA may have been transferred through touch, e.g. in the residue of cells from skin or sweat left in a fingerprint. Given its increased sensitivity, DNA LCN can be a particularly useful tool for investigating serious crimes where other profiling techniques have been exhausted or where options for forensic evidence appear to be limited. For example, when there is a very small amount of material present. DNA LCN takes longer than routine DNA profiling techniques, but it can provide extremely valuable intelligence for the police.

One of DNA LCN's most effective uses is in 'cold case reviews' – reviews of crimes from the past which have remained unsolved. The technique allows the FSS to re-test historic samples that have previously failed to yield a DNA profile. For example, Marion Crofts was raped and killed in 1981. At the time, DNA testing techniques were not sensitive enough to obtain a DNA profile of her killer. Microscope slides were deliberately left untouched in the hope that techniques would eventually become sensitive enough to obtain a profile. After nearly 20 years, a DNA LCN profile was obtained from Tony Jasinskyj which matched samples taken from Marion's clothing. He was convicted and jailed for life in 2002.

a) Which type of industry is most likely to use the Forensic Science Service? ....

b) How has DNA profiling improved over the last twenty years? ....

c) What does DNA LCN stand for and how is it different from standard DNA testing techniques?

....

d) Suggest one disadvantage of DNA LCN compared to standard DNA testing techniques.

....

e) How has the Forensic Science Service been able to use this technique to solve crimes that took place years ago?

....

f) Why did scientists decide to keep the samples from the Marion Crofts murder, even though their initial attempts to produce a DNA profile from them had failed?

....

Interpreting Information

Scientific Detection (cont.)

2 a) What is the pH scale, opposite, used to measure?

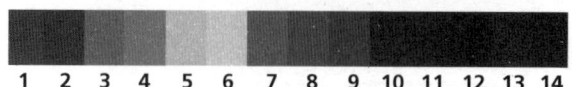

| 1 2 3 4 5 6 7 8 9 10 11 12 13 14 |

b) i) What is the range of values that represent acids?

....

ii) What is the range of values that represent alkalis?

....

iii) What is the pH of a neutral substance?

....

3 The image opposite shows a tick as viewed through a microscope.

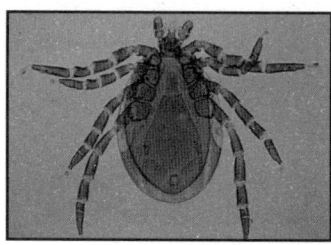

a) Write a short description of the tick shown, identifying its important features. (Hint: Include information that would help someone else to identify the tick without having the image to refer to.)

....

....

....

b) If the body length of the tick is 72mm, and the image has been enlarged to the scale 30mm:1mm, calculate the actual size of the tick.

....

c) Use the table below to identify the type of tick shown. Circle the correct variety.

Variety of Tick	Body Length (mm)
American dog tick	5.35–6.35
Lone star tick	5.35–6.35
Black-legged tick	2.15–3.15
Brown dog tick	3.80–4.80

Scientific Detection (cont.)

4 Below are the instructions that come with a home pregnancy test kit. Read them carefully.

> Remove the cap. Hold the test stick pointing downwards, and place the tip in your urine stream for 5 seconds. Lie the test stick flat until a blue line has appeared in the control window (this will take approximately 1 minute). If a line appears in the result window as well as the control window, you are pregnant. If there is a line in the control window only, you are not pregnant.

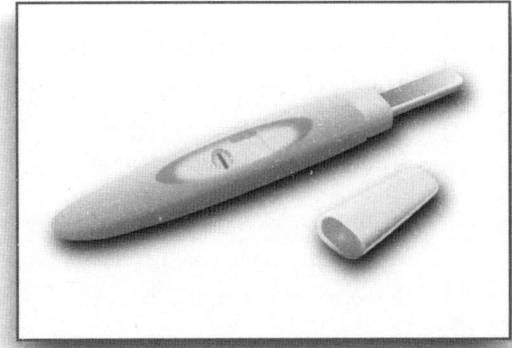

a) Does the pregnancy test stick above show a positive result or a negative result? ....

b) Why is it important for the test stick to have a control window?

....

Harnessing Chemicals

1 The two graphs below show the rate of a reaction using two different methods of measurement.

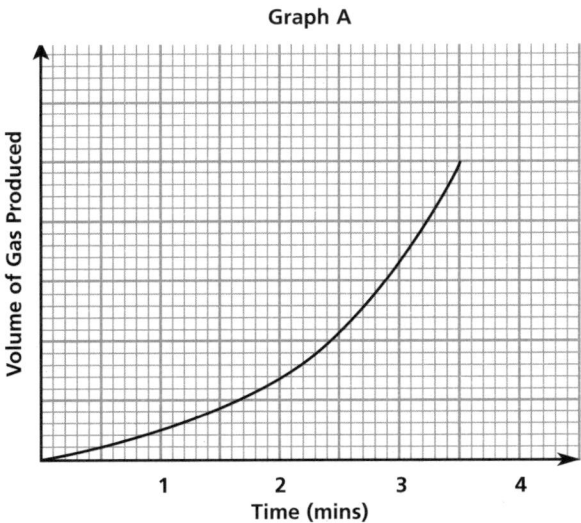

Graph A

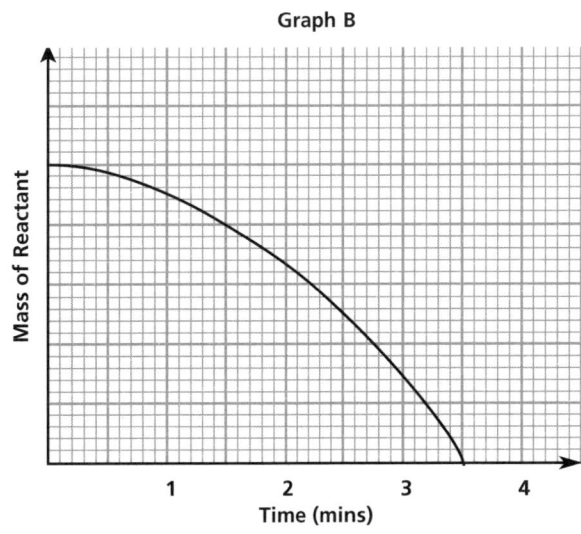

Graph B

a) How long does it take for the reaction to go to completion?

....

b) Explain, in as much detail as you can, why the graphs produce opposite curves.

....

Interpreting Information

Harnessing Chemicals (cont.)

2 Read the following information about ammonia before answering the questions below.

> Ammonia is one of the most highly produced inorganic chemicals in the world. It has many uses, but nearly 80% is used in agricultural fertilizers. Modern chemical plants use the Haber Process to produce ammonia. The reactants used are nitrogen (from the air) and hydrogen (from natural gas). An iron catalyst is used in the reaction.
>
> Temperature and pressure conditions affect the efficiency of the Haber Process. Increasing the pressure results in a higher yield of ammonia. However, very high pressures need strong and expensive equipment. Increasing the temperature increases the rate of reaction, but it also decreases the yield of ammonia.
>
> The Haber Process produces 500 million tonnes of artificial fertilizer per year. This fertilizer sustains 40% of the Earth's population. 1% of the world's energy supply is consumed in the manufacturing of that fertilizer.
>
> Ammonia is not normally hazardous to humans and other mammals. However, even when diluted, it is highly toxic to aquatic animals.

a) i) Why do you think a catalyst is used in the Haber Process?

_____

ii) Give one advantage of being able to use iron as the catalyst.

_____

b) i) What conditions would you need in order to produce the highest yield of ammonia possible?

_____

ii) Are these conditions economically viable for use in industry? Explain your answer.

_____

c) In terms of sustainability, list three problems associated with ammonia and the Haber Process.

i) _____

ii) _____

iii) _____

Harnessing Chemicals (cont.)

3 Carefully read the following information about the bulk production of sodium hydroxide before answering the questions below. You will also have to use your existing scientific knowledge.

> Sodium hydroxide is produced through a process called electrolysis which takes place in a 'cell'. An electric current is passed between two charged electrodes, through an aqueous solution of sodium chloride. Sodium hydroxide is formed at the negatively charged electrode (cathode) and chlorine is formed at the positively charged electrode (anode).
>
> It is important to stop the NaOH and Cl_2 from reacting together. There are three principal ways of doing this:
>
> **Mercury cell process** – a cathode made of mercury is used, and an amalgam of sodium metal is formed. The sodium is then reacted with water to produce NaOH. Mercury is a toxic chemical and there have been concerns about mercury contamination in plants which use this method.
>
> **Diaphragm cell process** – the anode is separated from the steel cathode by a permeable diaphragm. The sodium chloride is introduced into the anode compartment and flows through the diaphragm into the cathode compartment. Diluted caustic soda leaves the cell. The caustic soda must then be condensed by an evaporative process, which uses about three tonnes of steam per tonne of caustic soda.
>
> **Membrane cell process** – this is similar to the diaphragm cell process, but a Nafion membrane is used to separate the cathode and anode reactions. Only sodium ions and a little water pass through the membrane. It produces a higher quality of NaOH and requires the least amount of electric energy. The amount of steam needed to condense the caustic soda is relatively small too (less than one tonne per tonne of caustic soda).

a) i) What substance is sodium hydroxide produced from? ....

ii) How do you think this helps to keep the overall cost of production down?

....

b) i) Name one other product of this process. ....

ii) Is this a useful product? Explain your answer.

....

iii) Do you think the production of another product is an advantage or a disadvantage? Explain your answer.

....

....

Interpreting Information

Harnessing Chemicals (cont.)

3 (Continued)

c) If you were the manager of a chemical plant, which method would you use to stop the products from reacting? Explain your answer in as much detail as you can.

....

....

....

....

4 The table below details several different types of anti-dandruff shampoo.

Shampoo*	Perfume	Ketoconazole %	Reaction to Body	Other Active Ingredients
Shampoo A	Citrus	1.2	Causes a scalp rash	Selenium sulfide
Shampoo B	Peppermint	1	Causes harsh stinging of the eyes	Zinc pyrithione
Shampoo C	None	0.8	No reaction	Tea tree oil
Shampoo D	Lavender	1.1	No reaction	Tar

*To be approved for use as an anti-dandruff shampoo, the shampoo must contain at least 1% of the active ingredient Ketoconazole and cause no adverse effects.

a) Would Shampoo B pass an anti-dandruff shampoo product formulation test? Explain your answer.

....

b) Would Shampoo D pass an anti-dandruff shampoo product formulation test? Explain your answer.

....

c) Shampoo C would not pass an anti-dandruff formulation test, but it could be marketed as a normal shampoo. But why might this shampoo not be a popular choice?

....

d) Tea tree oil is an antibacterial ingredient which helps to stop skin from becoming infected. Would shampoo C or shampoo D be more effective at stopping infection?

....

Harnessing Chemicals (cont.)

5 Some chemicals are sold to laboratories as follows:

Sulfuric acid £7.30 per litre	Sodium hydroxide £28.60 per kilogram

An experiment was undertaken using 125cm³ sulfuric acid and 9g sodium hydroxide to make sodium sulfate.

a) What is the cost of the sulfuric acid that was used in the reaction above?

....

b) What is the cost of the sodium hydroxide that was used in the reaction above?

....

HT

6 The table below shows the solubility of various chemicals. If solubility is below 1, the chemical is insoluble in water. If solubility is above 1, the chemical is soluble in water.

Chemical	Formula	Solubility mol/dm³ at 20°C
Sodium carbonate	Na_2CO_3	0.66
Calcium carbonate	$CaCO_3$	0.00013
Zinc carbonate	$ZnCO_3$	0.00164
Sodium sulfate	Na_2SO_4	0.303
Zinc sulfate	$ZnSO_4$	3.56
Sodium nitrate	$NaNO_3$	12.3
Silver nitrate	$AgNO_3$	14.2
Silver chloride	$AgCl$	0.0000153

a) List three chemicals that could be made by the precipitation method.

i) .... **ii)** .... **iii)** ....

b) List three chemicals that could not be made by the precipitation method.

i) .... **ii)** .... **iii)** ....

Interpreting Information

Communications

1 The incomplete flow chart below shows the process of data transmission for a television broadcast.

```
[_____] → Encoding → Transmitter → Receiver → Decoding → [_____] →
```

a) Fill in the input and output stages in the diagram.

b) Suggest what the receiver stage could be.

_____

Materials and Performance

1 The table below details different materials and their properties

	Resistance to Corrosion	Cost to Manufacture	Density	Strength	Thermal Conductivity	Stiffness
Steel	Rusts	Cheap	High	Very high	High	High
Wood	Rots	Cheap	Medium	Low	Low	Medium high
Iron	Corrodes easily	Cheap	High	Brittle	High	High
Copper	Corrodes slowly	Expensive	High	Low	Very high	Low
Aluminium	Corrodes slowly	Moderately expensive	Low	Low	High	Medium
Glass	Corrodes slowly	Cheap	Low	Medium	Low	Very high

a) Strips of material can be used to build a bridge.

 i) Which material do you think would be suitable for building a small bridge over a stream? Explain your answer.

 _____

 ii) Which material do you think would be suitable for building a large bridge over a river that will be carrying cars? Explain your answer.

 _____

b) Would wood be a suitable material for making a saucepan? Explain your answer.

_____

c) Would there be any disadvantages in using copper to make saucepans? Explain your answer.